100 WRITING LESSONS

Narrative • Descriptive • Expository • Persuasive

Ready-to-Use Lessons to Help Students Become Strong Writers and Succeed on the Tests

Tara McCarthy

Formerly published as *Expository Writing*, *Descriptive Writing*, *Narrative Writing*, and *Persuasive Writing*

SCHOLASTIC

New York • Toronto • London • Auckland • Sydney
Mexico City • New Delhi • Hong Kong • Buenos Aires

Cover design by Jorge J. Namerow

Interior design by Teresa B. Southwell

Interior illustrations by Teresa B. Southwell

Editor: Sarah Glasscock

Copyeditor: David Klein

ISBN-13 978-0-545-11002-0

ISBN-10 0-545-11002-5

Copyright © 2009 by Tara McCarthy

All right reserved. Published by Scholastic Inc.

Printed in the U.S.A.

5 6 7 8 9 10 40 14 13 12

Contents

Expository Writing

Introduction

The imperative: Like musicians, writers have to practice every day to keep up their "chops." But how do you make room for writing—every day—amidst all the other goals you've set for your students?

One solution: Use the Descriptive, Narrative, Expository, and Persuasive writing lessons in this book. After introducing a lesson, then you can hand it over to students to complete and assess themselves. Are the lessons in this book going to make your students masters of each type of writing? Absolutely not! But what the lessons will do is provide an introduction to, review of, and practice in the basic steps as outlined for each section below.

How This Book Is Organized

I've pared the basics of each type of writing down to several essential concepts, and the lessons in each part correspond to a concept. Naturally, there is some overlapping between the parts. For example, in the Expository section, the dictum of Who-What-When-Where-Why-How appears more than once, as does the idea of centering on a main idea. (My late, great mentor, Paul Brandwine, called this "useful redundancy.") Each teaching page is accompanied by a reproducible.

Boxed tips on the teaching page offer general teaching tips, as well as approaches for ESL students, students who have special learning modalities, and those who need additional practice with the task.

Wind-Up lessons appear at the end of each writing section, and your input and assessment are important here. In many cases, students are asked to work on a fleshed-out final product.

The On Your Own activities at the end of each writing section provide ways for your students to apply their writing skills imaginatively. Use these pages with students who are "ready to fly." The final On Your Own activity, called Rate Yourself, is a self-assessment page for students.

Two Composition activities with reproducibles appear at the end of each of the Descriptive, Narrative, and Persuasive Writing sections. These are followed by an Across the Curriculum activity and reproducible tied to a different subject area.

ADDITIONAL SUGGESTIONS FOR USING THE LESSONS

1. Ask your students to write by hand. Though they may be used to working on computers to compose their work, I advise against it for the activities in this book. Here's why: On a computer, a writer tends to carefully edit each sentence or paragraph before going on to the next one. While this can be useful in some situations, it can be counterproductive for the activities here. What we're aiming for in general is a free flow, and that's best engendered by writing the entire piece by hand. Later, when the draft is done, students can go back and amend it. Those who wish to do so can use the computer to produce their final copies.

2. Stress to your students that teachers and adults face writing challenges, too. Participate with your students in carrying out some of these writing activities. Invite them to critique your writing.

3. Encourage students to read aloud their work. Sharing one's work and hearing the work of others makes ideas come to life, and helps students gain a deeper understanding and appreciation of the craft of writing.

4. Help students use what they've learned from the lessons in this book. Refer them to activities they've completed when they're grappling for a way to approach a science or social studies report.

5. Discuss tough stuff with students. It's not always easy to write, especially if you want to be a really good writer. Pose the following open-ended questions to your class:

   ➡ *What's the toughest thing about writing?*

   ➡ *What's the most rewarding part of writing?*

   ➡ *Good writers may revise several times before they feel satisfied with their work.*
   How do you know when a piece of your own writing is ready to present to your audience?

   ➡ *Who is the final judge of your writing: you or your audience?*

   ➡ *A great writer once said, "How do I know what I think until I see what I say?"*
   How does writing help you know what you think?

KEEP IN MIND . . .

➡ The activities in this book follow a sequence of instruction that I think you'll find valuable, but you can certainly veer from this sequence to fit the needs of your class. For instance, you may want to use a specific activity as a warm-up for a larger writing task you're assigning rather than using it in the sequence suggested here.

➡ Don't do fine-line corrections of your students' work. These lessons are designed as start-ups and practices, not as final products to be graded. Again, the object is to get students to write every day so that they come to see writing as a natural way of exploring and developing a topic. The practice will pay off later in the formal assignments and standardized tests your students will undertake.

Overview of the Four Writing Sections

DESCRIPTIVE WRITING

Part 1: Exploring Sensory Imagery

During the days or weeks in which your students are exploring sensory images, make the classroom itself an exploration site. Tell students how you will do this: Each day before school starts, you'll change the room in some way that is easy for most students to detect at first, and then in more subtle ways as the days go by. Students should look or listen (or even sniff!) for the change as they enter the room, then name it when the whole class is together.

Part 2: Choosing Words That Work

Make words a visible part of your classroom. As your students build their descriptive vocabulary, gradually decorate the room with banners, flags, labels, and posters that present words and phrases in fun, eye-catching ways. You might start by selecting from each student's portfolio or writing folder a particularly fine phrase or sentence, lettering it in color on a long strip of paper and then displaying the strips over the chalkboard or bulletin board.

Part 3: Organizing Descriptive Paragraphs

In writing and in formal speaking, *unity* means that all the parts relate to the whole. *Coherence* means that all the parts flow together, fit together, and follow one another in a logical way that readers can understand. Can young writers begin to understand and reach for the classic goals of unity and coherence?

Both unity and coherence call for organization. The activities in Part 3 show students how to use the descriptive writing techniques they've tried in Parts 1 and 2 to organize unified and coherent paragraphs, stories, and personal sketches.

NARRATIVE WRITING

Part 1: Writing Narratives About Our Own Experiences

Almost every day, students narrate aloud many stories based on their personal experiences. Because telling about our own experiences orally is such a natural part of our everyday lives, *writing* about them makes a comfortable introduction to written narratives in general. The activities in this section ease students into narrative writing by encouraging them to focus on what they know best: themselves.

Part 2: Writing Narratives About Other People

An other-oriented focus is vital for young writers. On both an affective and a cognitive level, the focus helps students appreciate the views and circumstances of real people with whom they come in contact in everyday life or in their curricular studies of the past. On an imaginative level, the focus encourages students to trust and use their writerly "what-if" instincts to try a variety of points of view as they develop their own stories.

Part 3: Writing Narratives About Literature

Writing a narrative about a particular book or story encourages students to think like the author did, to get into that author's shoes by extending or elaborating on the existing narrative. The approach is similar to one that art students use when they set up an easel before a great painting, replicate or reinterpret it, and thereby learn the techniques used by the artist. Unlike a report about a book, which comes from the "outside," a narrative about a book comes from the "inside," from the student writer's participation in the story.

Part 4: Writing Stories

To write original narratives that satisfy both themselves and their readers, students must integrate the elements of character, plot, and setting. If your students have carried out all or some of the major activities in Parts 1, 2, and 3, they are prepared to investigate these elements in more depth as they write their own stories.

EXPOSITORY WRITING

How do you carry off the goal of writing daily with expository writing, a genre that requires the mastery of the following traditional steps?

- State your main idea.
- Develop your main idea by listing essential facts in order.
- Direct your writing to a specific audience.

I've pared the basics of expository writing down to four parts that build upon each other:

Part 1: Main Idea

Part 2: Purpose

Part 3: Audience

Part 4: Presentation

PERSUASIVE WRITING

Part 1: Exploring the Elements of Persuasion

The lessons in this section are warm-ups. You can use them to introduce or review the major elements of persuasive writing with your students. You can also use the outcomes of these lessons to informally assess students' prior knowledge and skill in using these elements.

Part 2: Analyzing Persuasive Techniques

As students become familiar with the basic elements of persuasion presented in Part 1, they grow in their ability to analyze the persuasive messages that they see, hear, and read every day. Prepare for Part 2 by setting up a classroom reference collection of mail-order catalogs and advertising flyers. Enlist student assistance in building this collection. If possible, also make a videotape of several TV commercials that use the techniques presented in the following pages. Ask students to use and build the collection as they carry out the activities in the section.

Part 3: Persuading for Different Purposes

Through the lessons in Parts 1 and 2, students have identified and practiced using the elements and techniques of persuasive writing. Part 3 lessons help students apply what they've learned to write persuasively in many different situations. Whatever the situation, the same general guidelines apply. Ahead of time, prepare the following SAY IT poster for display, and remind students to refer to it as they write.

Guidelines for Persuasive Writing

S   STATE YOUR SUBJECT.

A   KNOW YOUR AUDIENCE.

Y   IDENTIFY YOURSELF.

I   KNOW YOUR INTENTION. WHY ARE YOU WRITING?

T   DECIDE ON THE TONE.

-- Tara McCarthy

Narrative Writing

Narrative Writing

Writing Narratives About Our Own Experiences: JOURNALS

Goal: Use journals to promote writing fluency.

➡ Get Set

For writers, journal entries are raw material for longer narratives. Show your students how to set up and keep different types of journals: double-entry, problem-solution, and partner journals. Distribute the reproducible on page 13.

➡ Go

Double-Entry Journal: Show students how to set up double-column pages. In the left Fact column, they write a fact about something that has happened to them, or about an event in a book they're reading (*note-taking*). In the right My Reaction column, students note their feelings or opinions about the event (*note-making*). Direct their attention to the examples on the reproducible.

Problem-Solution Journal: Point out the format of this type of journal on the reproducible. In the left column, students state a real-life problem or a problem in a book they're reading. In the right column, they write one or more ways the problem might be solved.

Partner Journal: Show students how to set up a three-column page with the following headings: Situation, My Notes, and My Partner's Ideas. In the Situation column, they record a fact about an event in real life or in a book. In the My Notes column, they state their reactions to or predictions about the event. Partners respond to those notes in the My Partner's Ideas column.

➡ Follow Up

Encourage students to review their journals at least once a week to jot down any story ideas they get from reviewing their entries. Explain that story-idea notes can be phrases, informal lists, or sentences, but they should always present events in time-sequence.

Tip Suggest that students add more columns to their Partner Journals. To continue the exchange between students and their partners, the fourth column could be labeled My Reaction to My Partner's Ideas, and the fifth column could be labeled More Ideas From My Partner.

Narrative Writing

100 Writing Lessons © by Tara McCarthy • Scholastic Teaching Resources

Name _____ Date _____

Writing Narratives About Our Own Experiences: JOURNALS

You can record your experiences, thoughts, and ideas in different kinds of journals.

Double-Entry Journal

FACT	MY REACTION
Tom Sawyer tricked his friends into whitewashing the fence for him.	I think Tom was smart. The job got done. But I wonder if Tom would like his friends to trick him!
My mom took my brother and me to an art exhibit.	I thought I'd be bored, but I wasn't. The exhibit was full of mobiles about circuses!

Problem-Solution Journal

PROBLEM	POSSIBLE SOLUTIONS
Our class has to read poems in a program for the whole school. The problem is that some kids get nervous when they have to speak to a large group.	Shy kids could participate by making posters or pictures about the poems classmates will read. Shy kids could practice reading a poem to just a few of us and then to more and more of us.
We're just looking at the first part of The Odyssey, where Ulysses is returning from the Trojan Wars. The problem is that Ulysses gets lost and can't find his way home.	Maybe Ulysses could just anchor his ship and wait for a captain of another ship to come along and give him directions. He could beg the goddess Athena to get him home safely.

Narrative Writing

Narrative Writing

Writing Narratives About Our Own Experiences:
OBSERVATION DIARIES

> Goal: Observe changes or sequences of events and narrate them sparely.

➡ Get Set

In an Observation Diary, the writer chooses an object or nonhuman entity in his or her immediate environment and notes briefly, over a two- or three-day period, what happens to the object or how it changes.

➡ Go

Explain what an Observation Diary is and then distribute the reproducible on page 15. Read aloud and discuss the sample Observation Diary entry about a pencil. Point out that the entry contains descriptive phrases as well as complete sentences.

Have students brainstorm a list of objects or animals they might observe for several days. Then ask each student to choose an item from the list to write about in an Observation Diary. To jump-start the process, suggest topics such as the following:

• sounds in my neighborhood
• a tree outside my window
• a particular sidewalk or street
• an ant colony or spider web
• a classroom aquarium

• a household pet
• a junk car in an empty lot
• the school corridor
• a swing in the playground
• a table in the classroom

• the school gym
• my favorite shoes
• the morning sky
• the sun, stars, moon
• birds at a bird feeder

➡ Follow Up

Ask students to use their Observation Diary entries to write a brief narrative paragraph that lists sequentially what they've observed.

Tip After students complete their paragraphs, have them form small Free-Read groups. In a Free-Read, the writer reads aloud to the group, and group members listen without commenting. During the reading, or just after, the writer makes notes about what to change in, add to, or delete from the draft. Because the Observation Diary doesn't focus on a student's private life as a traditional diary does, entries can be shared without raising privacy issues.

Narrative Writing

Name _____ Date _____

Writing Narratives About Our Own Experiences: OBSERVATION DIARIES

A. In an Observation Diary, the writer observes an object in the environment and makes notes about it for several days. Here's a sample.

> OBSERVING MY PENCIL
>
> MONDAY: Nice and sharp and long and new. This pencil is ready to go! It had to get sharpened after lunch, because it had to write spelling words in the morning. So now it's shorter. Oops! Point got broken while drawing a map this afternoon.
>
> TUESDAY: Pencil got lost in my desk for a while. Found under a pile of old lunch bags. Pencil looks stubby, and there is peanut butter on it.
>
> WEDNESDAY: Sharpened pencil. But what happened to the eraser end? Now it's stubby! Pencils require a lot of attention!

B. Observe an object in your environment for a few days. Record your findings in an Observation Diary.

> OBSERVING MY _____
>
> TUESDAY:
>
> WEDNESDAY:
>
> THURSDAY:
>
> FRIDAY:

Narrative Writing

Writing Narratives About Our Own Experiences: LOGS

Goal: Record information in a log and narrate findings in sequence.

➡ Get Set

Keeping a log is a closure activity: Students write a sequential listing of information that applies only to a specific situation or task that has been defined beforehand.

Explain to students what a log is. List people who routinely keep logs, and ask students to determine the major questions each of those log-keepers wants to answer. For example, *Ship captain: What progress does my ship make day-by-day? School nurse: Which students came to my office today? What were their problems? Building guard: Who wanted to enter the building tonight? What was their purpose? What was my response?*

➡ Go

Distribute the reproducible on page 17. Ask students to note the title of the sample log and read the entries aloud. Then ask them to tell what sequence the log uses (time sequence: date and time). Pose the following question: *How would this log help the log-keeper write a story about a hurricane?*

With the class, brainstorm a list of subjects that invite regular log entries over a period of a week or two. Have students work independently or with a partner or small group to choose a subject, prepare a Log Notebook, and write entries at regular intervals. Remind students that each entry should begin with the date and time. Here are some sample topics:

- weather conditions over a week's time
- personal response to reading a novel or chapter book
- steps taken in getting to know a new classmate
- the progress of a class or community project

➡ Follow Up

Ask students to use their Log Notebooks to write one or more narrative paragraphs about the subject.

Tip You may want to create a model paragraph based on the sample log on the reproducible to share with students.

Narrative Writing

Name _____ Date _____

Writing Narratives About Our Own Experiences: LOGS

A. A log is a written record of events recorded in sequence. Here's a sample.

LOG: What Happens as the Hurricane Approaches Our Town?

Date/Time	Events
9-6-08/6 a.m.	Weather forecasters say storm will hit our area in about 5 hours. Homeowners and storekeepers hammer boards over windows and doors.
9-6-08/7 a.m.	Strong winds are kicking up. Big waves hit beaches. Sun hidden as dark, angry clouds move in fast.

B. Prepare a Log Notebook for a topic of your choice. Record several entries every day for a week. Remember to begin each entry with the date and time of the event.

LOG: _____

Date/Time	Events

100 Writing Lessons © by Tara McCarthy • Scholastic Teaching Resources

Narrative Writing

Writing Narratives About Our Own Experiences: AUTOBIOGRAPHICAL INCIDENTS

Goal: Examine an experience to discover what has been learned from it.

➡ Get Set

Explain that an autobiographical incident narrates a personal experience that occurred over a brief span of time: a few minutes or hours, or—at the most—a day or two. As in most narratives, the events in the incident are presented in sequence. The writer adds his or her sensory impressions and shares his or her feelings with the reader.

➡ Go

To help students understand that brief, simple incidents can have a powerful affect, read aloud the example on the reproducible on page 19. Discuss students' reactions to the incident. What sensory impressions and feelings does the writer share?

➡ Follow Up

Ask each student to jot down subjects or titles for three or four autobiographical incidents, such as the following: *New school—I was scared; then met new friend* or *lost in shopping mall when I was 4 years old.* Then have each student choose one subject and produce a rough draft of the autobiographical incident. If they're having trouble thinking of an incident, suggest they answer one of the prompts on the reproducible.

Tip Stress that an autobiographical incident doesn't have to deal with an earth-shaking, newspaper-worthy event. It just has to be important to the writer.

Narrative Writing

Name _____ Date _____

Writing Narratives About Our Own Experiences: AUTOBIOGRAPHICAL INCIDENTS

A. An autobiographical incident tells about a personal experience that happened over a short period of time. The events are told in time-sequence, and the writer adds his or her sensory impressions and feelings. Here's a sample.

Outside the house where we lived when I was a little girl, there was a birch tree that had been bent over by many winter storms. In the summer, the leaves of the bending tree trailed on the ground and formed a little tent. I called it my Reading Tree, because I would sit under the leafy boughs and read my books. It was a green, cool, and private place, and I loved it very much.

One summer day, I came home from a picnic with my friends—and my Reading Tree was gone! All that was left was a short, sawed-off, sad-looking stump! I burst into tears.

My dad came running out of the house. "What's wrong?" he asked.

Pointing to the stump, I bawled, "My Reading Tree! My Reading Tree!"

"Oh, Sweetie," my father said, "we had to cut it down because it had a disease that could infect other trees. You understand, don't you?"

I nodded my head, but I didn't really understand then. And even now—when I do understand—I still miss my Reading Tree.

B. Write your own autobiographical incident. You can answer any of the following prompts if you need help getting started:

- Close your eyes. Visualize a still life or photo from your past. People and objects are frozen in time. Now tell what your still life shows.
- Close your eyes. Imagine that you're watching a movie of an event from your past. Now tell what your movie shows.
- Close your eyes and think of these four words that name feelings: *sad, puzzled, happy, angry.* Now tell about a time when you had one of these feelings.

Writing Narratives About Our Own Experiences: WIND-UP

Ask students to look at the journals, observation diaries, and logs they completed in this section and select a topic they want to expand into an autobiographical incident. They will carry this narrative through the writing process.

In addition to relating the facts, observations, sequence of events, and ideas, students will also need to focus on describing the environment and their own responses. Encourage them to use the reproducible on page 21 to help create their narrative.

Students may accompany their narratives with photos, drawings, maps, excerpts from the selected journal, diary, or log, or other graphics.

Encourage students to publish their work by tape-recording it, forming discussion groups around common topics represented in their narratives, or by performing pantomimes or skits.

Narrative Writing

Name _____ Date _____

Writing Narratives About Our Own Experiences: WIND-UP

Write an autobiographical incident based on an entry from your journal, observation diary, or log.

My autobiographic incident will be about _____ .
I'll use the entry from my _____ to write about the incident.

After deciding upon your entry, close your eyes and think about writing it. Jot your sensory impressions, feelings, and steps or events below.

Where were you when you wrote your entry? Use your senses: What did you see, hear, smell, touch, taste?

How did you feel when you were writing your entry? Did it make you remember any other experiences you've had?

Describe, in order, the sequence, events, steps.

100 Writing Lessons © by Tara McCarthy • Scholastic Teaching Resources

Narrative Writing

Writing Narratives About Other People:
FIRST-PERSON BIOGRAPHIES

> Goal: Focus on how one person or character influences another.

➡ Get Set

A first-person biography narrates an incident involving the writer and someone he or she knows personally. An exemplary first-person biography shows something important about the focus character *and* shows how this character has affected the writer's life or ideas.

➡ Go

Distribute the reproducible on page 23. Define a first-person biography and read aloud the sample first-person biography on the reproducible. Use the sample to discuss a biography's key points:

- Describes main character
- Narrates the interaction between main character and writer
- Tells what the writer has learned from the interaction

Have students work independently to list family members, friends, teachers, neighbors, or people encountered by chance who have affected or influenced their views. Then ask them to work with a partner or in a small group to tell *why* or *how* these people were influential.

➡ Follow Up

Tell students to write a rough draft of a first-person biography. Assure them that the only standard that they will be judged on is that the draft be neat and clear enough for the writer to read back smoothly to an audience of four or five classmates. Then instruct students how to use a Say-Back Response in which the writer reads his or her draft and then asks the listeners to "say back" in their own words what the writer is getting at. Writers can use questions such as, "What do you hear me saying? What are some ideas you have for helping me say it better?"

Tip Say-backs are valuable when students are at the early stages of framing a narrative and are looking for a main idea to focus on.

Narrative Writing

Name _____ Date _____

Writing Narratives About Other People:
FIRST-PERSON BIOGRAPHIES

A first-person biography narrates an incident involving the writer and someone he or she knows. Here's an example.

Mr. Ames

Mr. Ames is known as the Neighborhood Grouch. He never answers when you speak to him. He always has a sort of frown on his face. He lives alone and never seems to have visitors.

"Mr. Ames is just so *unfriendly*," said my mom.

"He's a total drag!" agreed my sister.

Describes main character.

One day, my Frisbee landed accidentally in Mr. Ames's garden. He was working out there, so I was a little afraid of retrieving the Frisbee.

Then Mr. Ames held up the Frisbee. "Here's your toy, Sonny," he said. He was smiling slightly.

"Thanks!" I said as I went to get the Frisbee. "I'm usually pretty good at aiming it, but a tiny breeze can throw it off-course."

"Eh? Eh?" asked Mr. Ames, cupping his hand to his ear.

Narrates interaction between main character and writer.

Suddenly I realized that Mr. Ames was totally deaf! No wonder he didn't reply to neighbors' greetings! No wonder he seemed unfriendly! He couldn't hear us!

That day I not only got my Frisbee back but also stayed to help Mr. Ames plant tomatoes. We communicated just fine through gestures and smiles.

So I learned that you can't always rely on other people's opinions. Often you have to check things out for yourself and form your own ideas. My idea of Mr. Ames is that he's a great guy and a good friend!

Tells what writer has learned from interaction.

---

100 Writing Lessons © by Tara McCarthy • Scholastic Teaching Resources

Narrative Writing

Writing Narratives About Other People:
FIRST-PERSON BIOGRAPHIES
BASED ON HISTORY

Goal: Understand the feelings and motives of other people and implement this understanding in writing narratives.

➡ Get Set

Through basal texts and related literature, students encounter figures from history whose exploits and achievements have a global significance. What can an "ordinary" person possibly share with these historical giants? Students find out by composing brief narratives in which they take the point of view of a historical figure.

➡ Go

Introduce the concept by reading aloud a statement that might have been made by a historical person your class is studying. Ask students to guess who the person is. Here's an example for Harriet Tubman:

You think it's easy to follow familiar paths? Not if it's slave territory! Believe me, I quaked at every step of every journey! I could be intercepted, captured, punished, returned to slavery at any time! You can call me courageous if you want. But I didn't feel courageous. I felt determined. I was determined to lead as many of my people as possible from slavery to freedom. But it was a scary task, every step of the way!

Hand out the reproducible on page 25. Have students brainstorm to complete the chart, noting major situations faced by the historical figures they've recently studied.

➡ Follow Up

Ask students to write a rough draft of one or two paragraphs based on one of the chart entries on the reproducible. Then have them read aloud their work in small groups.

Tip Groups can use the Free-Read strategy on p. 14 or try Mental Movie, in which the writer reads aloud and listeners close their eyes and envision what the words make them see. Listeners reveal what they see in their Mental Movies, but make no other comments.

Narrative Writing

Name _____ Date _____

Writing Narratives About Other People:
FIRST-PERSON BIOGRAPHIES
BASED ON HISTORY

A. Think of historical figures you've been studying. How would they think and feel in certain situations? Finish completing the chart, using their first-person viewpoint.

REAL-LIFE PERSON	
Amelia Earhart	Flying west over the Pacific Ocean.
	My copilot and I have never felt so
	lost and alone.

B. Now choose one of the people you've been studying and write a first-person biography about him or her.

_____

_____

_____

_____

_____

_____

_____

_____

Narrative Writing

Writing Narratives About Other People:
IF ONLY THEY COULD SPEAK–
UNUSUAL NARRATORS

Goal: Expand knowledge of point of view and demonstrate this understanding.

➡ Get Set

What did Amelia Earhart's plane think about? What did Columbus's Santa Maria feel as she was tossed about on the wild Atlantic? What thoughts might the hidden paths and safe houses have had as they were inhabited by the people Harriet Tubman guided to freedom? Questions like these provide valuable practice for young writers as they learn how to consider events and people from different points of view.

➡ Go

Introduce the concept by having students brainstorm a list of familiar items from their lives, such as my lunch box, the school bus, my cat Mitzie, the refrigerator, and so on.

Next, show what you think one of the items on the list would say. For example the refrigerator might say, "Open, close! Open, close! On and off goes my light! These people are always looking for stuff to eat!"

Challenge students to help you draft a paragraph told from the point of view of another "speaker" from the list. Scribe the paragraph on the board.

➡ Follow Up

Distribute the reproducible on page 27. Help students brainstorm to add things to the list that relate to the historical events they've been studying. Have individuals or partners choose one of the nonhuman entities and write about the historical incident from its point of view.

Tip As the class works on the paragraph, intercede as necessary with the following statements: "You are telling this from something's point of view. Imagine that you are this 'something.' How would this 'something' say it?" Emphasize where the words *I*, *me*, *my*, and *mine* establish the first-person point of view.

Narrative Writing

Name _____ Date _____

100 Writing Lessons © by Tara McCarthy • Scholastic Teaching Resources

Writing Narratives About Other People:
IF ONLY THEY COULD SPEAK– UNUSUAL NARRATORS

A. Think of the historical events and incidents you've been studying. What kinds of animals or objects were involved in them? Add those to the list below.

Paul Revere's horse	Thomas Edison's first lightbulb
Mary Shelley's desk where she	Sojourner Truth's cat
wrote <u>Frankenstein</u>	Sacagawea's canoe as she guided
The Hudson River as ships from	explorers through the Northwest
Europe began to explore it	A dinosaur fossil being dug up by
	a paleontologist

B. Now, choose one of the entries from the chart and write about the historical event or incident from that point of view.

_____

_____

_____

_____

_____

_____

_____

_____

Writing Narratives About Other People:
PICTURE-PROMPT NARRATIVES

Goal: Create imaginative narratives.

➡ Get Set

You can use great photos and reproductions of fine art to stimulate students' narrative imagination. Choose a collection of pictures that show people in action or exhibiting strong feelings.

➡ Go

Display a photo or painting. Model the activity by telling a brief story inspired by it. This example is based on the ballet paintings of Edouard Degas.

This is a painting by Edouard Degas. It shows a ballet dancer lacing up her toe shoes. I imagine this story when I look at the painting:

The dancer's name is Sophie. She's very nervous! This will be her first public performance. All her family and friends are in the audience. Sophie wonders, "Will I be okay? Will I do every step right?" Sophie goes onstage. She is perfect! She bows and smiles. "This is the life for me!" she says to herself.

Hand out the reproducible on page 29. Then ask pairs of students to choose another picture from the collection, discuss what it shows, and record ideas about the story or stories it suggests on the reproducible.

➡ Follow Up

Ask students to write short narratives based on the charts they made with their partners. Remind them to refer to the picture itself for additional ideas and details.

Tip Suggest that partners use the Writer's Right strategy. In this technique, the author tells his or her partner exactly what to listen for. For example: "I'd like you to listen to the descriptions in my story." The listener then provides only the feedback the writer has asked for.

Narrative Writing

Name _____ Date _____

Writing Narratives About Other People:
PICTURE-PROMPT NARRATIVES

A. Choose a picture. Discuss it with a partner. What story does the picture tell? Write your ideas in the chart.

Title of Painting or Photo:	What It Shows
Artist or Photographer:	**Ideas for Stories**

B. Now, use the chart to help you write a short narrative story about the picture. Work on your own and then share your story with your partner.

_____

_____

_____

_____

_____

_____

_____

_____

Writing Narratives About Other People: WIND-UP

Ask students to imagine that they could correspond with a historical figure or an animal or object connected to that person. For example, what would they want to know about Meriwether Lewis's journey across the country? Or what would students ask Lewis's dog about the trek? Conversely, what might Lewis want to know about students' camping trips or scouting adventures? Or what might his dog want to know about students' pets?

Once students have made a selection and written their letters, have them exchange letters with a partner. Each student will then respond, in character, to the letter. Encourage pairs to continue the correspondence through two or three exchanges.

Narrative Writing

Name _____ Date _____

Writing Narratives About Other People: WIND-UP

A. Think about the historical events you've been studying. Suppose you could write a letter to someone involved in one of the events. What would you want to know? Which details of your own life would you want to share? Or if you'd like to know more about an object or an animal connected to that person, you can write to it instead.

Use the form below, or copy it on a sheet of paper.

Date

Dear

Sincerely,

B. Exchange your letter with a partner. Take on the voice of the person—or object or animal—your partner has written to and answer the letter. Use the form below, or copy it on a sheet of paper.

Date

Dear

Sincerely,

100 Writing Lessons © by Tara McCarthy • Scholastic Teaching Resources

Narrative Writing

Writing Narratives About Literature:
STORY SUMMARIES

> Goal: Recall major elements in a story.

➡ Get Set

An exemplary story summary briefly states the main steps in the plot in sequence and names the main characters. Instructing your class in how to write a summary may be time-consuming, but it pays off in big ways later on by providing the background students need to write independently about literature.

➡ Go

Start with a whole-class brainstorm. With you as scribe at the chalkboard, students briefly describe what happened in a familiar story. (Leave lots space between each line of the developing paragraph.) Then reframe the five questions on the reproducible on page 33 and pose them to students. Based on the answers, cross out any unnecessary information, circle any out-of-sequence phrases or sentences, and draw arrows to where they belong. Then write vital additions above the appropriate lines, and combine sentences.

➡ Follow Up

Distribute the reproducible on page 33. Have the class brainstorm a list of titles of stories they've recently read, then ask each student to work independently to write a rough-draft summary of one of the stories.

Tip Suggest that students write numerals (1, 2, 3, etc.) next to each event in their summaries and check to make sure this shows the order in which things really happened in the story. If an event is out of order in the summary, they can circle it and use an arrow to show where it belongs.

100 Writing Lessons © by Tara McCarthy • Scholastic Teaching Resources

Name _____ Date _____

Writing Narratives About Literature:
STORY SUMMARIES

A. The best story summary does the following:

- States only the main events and states them in the order they happened
- Includes the names of the main characters
- Combines ideas whenever possible
- Gives all the essential information as briefly as possible

Cinderella wants to go the king's ball, but her stepmother and stepsisters won't let her. Cinderella's godmother provides her with a dress and a carriage, and Cinderella goes to the ball. The Prince falls in love with her. Leaving the ball, Cinderella loses her glass slipper. The Prince searches everywhere for the woman whom the slipper will fit. He finally finds Cinderella. The shoe fits, and the Prince marries her.

B. Summarize a story you've read recently. After you've finished, answer the following questions. Based on the answers, revise your summary if necessary.

1. Did you include any unnecessary information in the summary?

2. Did you give the information in order?

3. Did you name all the key characters?

4. Did you leave out any important plot information?

5. Can you state any of the key information more briefly?

Narrative Writing

Writing Narratives About Literature:
BOOK CHARACTER CONVERSATIONS

> **Goal:** Focus on characters in a story.

➡ Get Set

A book-character conversation is modeled on a TV interview show. The interviewer (you, or in a follow-up, a savvy student) poses questions to characters from different stories who have much in common.

➡ Go

On the board, start a chart that notes a common characteristic of characters in different stories and relevant major questions the interviewer might ask.

CHARACTERISTIC	INTERVIEWEES	INTERVIEWER'S PROMPTS
Courage	<u>Winnie the Pooh</u>: went up in a balloon to get honey <u>Sam</u> in <u>My Side of the Mountain</u>: lived alone in the wilderness <u>Gretel</u> in "Hansel and Gretel": fooled the witch and saved her brother	What was courageous about what you did? What happened? What is your advice to someone who might want to try the same thing? Winnie, Sam, and Gretel, share with us your ideas about what courage is.

➡ Follow Up

Hand out the reproducible on page 35 and have students complete their own charts. Then invite groups of students to take turns choosing roles and acting out the interviews they've outlined on their charts.

> **Tip** If possible, tape-record the finished interviews and provide time for the class to listen to them. Use this directed-listening prompt: "Listen to discover what these book characters have in common and how they are different."

Narrative Writing

Name _____ Date _____

Writing Narratives About Literature:
BOOK CHARACTER CONVERSATIONS

Think of a characteristic that characters in several different stories might share, such as exhibiting courage or being a good friend. If you interviewed these characters, what would you ask them? Complete the chart.

CHARACTERISTIC	INTERVIEWEES	INTERVIEWER'S PROMPTS

Narrative Writing

Writing Narratives About Literature:
DIFFERENT VOICES

Goal: Consider story events from the viewpoints of different characters in the story.

➡ Get Set

Explain that in a well-told story, all the major characters come alive because the writer has thought deeply about what each of them is like. When young writers emulate this valuable prewriting process, they not only gain insights into a book or story they've read but also find ways to develop and enrich their own stories.

➡ Go

Distribute the reproducible on page 37 and discuss the excerpt from the Poe story and the examples showing the viewpoints of the other characters in the story. Then review a story students have read that is told from the first-person point of view. Work with students to retell a part of that story from the point of view of another character and record the results on the board.

➡ Follow Up

Ask each student to choose another character from a book he or she has read and narrate a key event from the "I" point of view. Have students produce a rough-draft paragraph to share with a group later.

Tip Pointing helps a writer decide if his or her main viewpoint is getting through to the audience. Before reading to the group, tell the writer to say, "Listen, then tell me which of my words or phrases stick in your mind. Just tell me what they are; don't explain why."

Narrative Writing

Name _____ Date _____

Writing Narratives About Literature:
DIFFERENT VOICES

This passage is an excerpt from the Edgar Allan Poe story "The Fall of the House of Usher." The events in the story are recounted from the point of view of the man who visits the gloomy home of Roderick Usher, his childhood friend. Here's what happens when the visitor sees Lady Madeline, Roderick's sister.

From "The Fall of the House of Usher" by Edgar Allan Poe
The Visitor speaks as "I."

"While he [Roderick Usher] spoke, the Lady Madeline . . . passed through . . . without having noticed my presence, disappeared. I regarded her with an utter astonishment not unmixed with dread. . . . When a door . . . closed upon her, my glance sought instinctively and eagerly the countenance of the brother, but he had buried his face in his hands, and I could only perceive . . . the emaciated fingers through which trickled many passionate tears."

In these passages, the writer imagines how Roderick Usher and Lady Madeline would relate the events from their points of view.

A Different Voice: Roderick Usher speaks as "I."

How could I explain to my childhood friend how despairing I was over my sister's illness? As Madeline appeared in the doorway, I realized again how frail and sick she was. I began to weep as I thought how empty my life would be without her.

A Different Voice: Madeline Usher speaks as "I."

Weak as I was, I still managed to go downstairs to peek at the visitor. I hoped he didn't see me! I knew I looked dreadfully ill. I returned to my room, comforted that my sad, lonely brother had a friend to talk to.

Narrative Writing

Writing Narratives About Literature:
ADDING TO THE STORY

> **Goal:** Focus on the plot and the logical progression of story events.

➡ Get Set

Most professional writers strive to show how one event flows believably from the events that precede it. By creating logical extensions of stories and books they've read, your students come to appreciate and utilize the task of plotting as they create their own stories.

➡ Go

Lead the class through a Let's-Imagine activity to help students brainstorm what might happen to a favorite character after the story concludes. Here are two suggestions to model:

- *Let's imagine that Wilbur, the pig in* <u>Charlotte's Web</u>, *has grown quite old and meets two new piglets in the barnyard. What might the piglets think or worry about, and how might Wilbur help them?*
- *Let's imagine that Rumpelstiltskin, stomping down to the center of the earth after the queen has guessed his name, meets another magical being who wants to help a human complete a task. How might Rumpelstiltskin help with the task, using the experience he had with the miller's daughter?*

➡ Follow Up

Pass out the reproducible on page 39. Ask pairs to collaborate on notes or an outline about an event that extends a story both students are familiar with. Partners then work independently to write a rough draft of the event and read their drafts to one another. Tell them to use the "Say-Back" method again to check that the sequence is clear. (see page 22).

Tip If students are stuck for ideas about how to get going, give them the following advice: "Just write, like you do in a Quickwrite. Fast and furiously, write about all the things that might happen in the episode you and your partner have outlined or made notes about."

Narrative Writing

Name _____ Date _____

Writing Narratives About Literature:
ADDING TO THE STORY

A. Think of a favorite story. Write the title and a summary of it below.

Title of Story: _____

Summary:

_____

_____

_____

_____

B. What might have happened to the main character after the story ended? Work with a partner to make notes or an outline about an event that continues the story.

C. Use your notes or outline to write a draft of the new story event on a separate sheet of paper.

Narrative Writing

Writing Narratives About Literature:
PUT YOURSELF IN THE STORY

Goal: Develop empathy for the central characters in a story and an understanding of how events affect behavior.

➡ Get Set

On the board, draw a chart like the one below. Fill in the first two columns to reflect a story the class knows well. Tell students that the first column names story characters they admire, the second column tells what admirable things the character has accomplished, and the third column gives students a chance to insert themselves into the story.

Story and Main Character	Accomplishment	Me in the Story
Cinderella	Poor and mistreated, she still manages to attend the royal ball, win the Prince's love, and eventually marry him.	Lisa (me!) is a guest at the king's ball. She advises Cinderella to leave a little token—like a glass shoe—so the Prince can find her.

➡ Go

Challenge students to imagine that they are a new character in the story who gets to help the main character accomplish his or her goal. Work with them in filling in the third column. Then distribute the reproducible on page 41. As the class thinks of other stories, have students complete the chart for those stories.

➡ Follow Up

Ask students to use their charts to rewrite a section of one of the stories to include themselves as part of the action. They can work independently or enlist a partner to help them.

Tip Some students may need this "TV-Jog" warm-up: "Think of a TV program that you enjoy. What episode was particularly interesting? Now imagine that you are an additional character in that episode. Write a narrative paragraph in which you take part in the action."

Narrative Writing

Name _____ Date _____

Writing Narratives About Literature:
PUT YOURSELF IN THE STORY

A. Think of some stories you know. Imagine you're a new character in these stories. You help this character accomplish goals, or talk with him or her. You can refer to yourself as I, or use your real name. Write your ideas in the chart.

Story and Main Character	Accomplishment	Me in the Story

B. Choose one of the stories. Use the ideas in your chart to rewrite a section of the story to include yourself!

_____

_____

_____

_____

_____

Narrative Writing

Writing Narratives About Literature:
NARRATING PERSONAL CONNECTIONS

> **Goal:** Make personal connections with the lives and experiences of book characters.

➡ Get Set

By writing about their personal connections to literature, students get practice in identifying *theme* in what they read, and in thinking about theme as they write their own stories.

➡ Go

Review the concept of theme with students. A theme is an idea that can be stated in a sentence and suggests a universal truth that applies to many real-life situations. Books often have more than one theme. Distribute the reproducible on page 43. Then, with the whole class or a small group, discuss one theme in a book that students have recently read and have students record it on the reproducible. Here are some examples:

BOOK TITLE	A THEME IN THE BOOK
The Moorchild (Eloise McGraw, McElderry, 1996)	Sometimes a person feels rejected by everyone around them, or so different that he or she doesn't fit in anywhere!
My Brother Sam Is Dead (Collier & Collier, Scholastic, 1974)	Family members may strongly disagree with one another about political and social issues.

Ask students to quickly write about a personal experience related to the theme.

➡ Follow Up

Suggest to students that they quietly read aloud their personal experience drafts, making marginal notes about what they'd like to change in a second draft. This is an apt place to review the composition skill of combining sentences (page 121).

> **Tip** You may want to mention to students that this activity is a form of Quickwrite. In both tasks, writers jot down everything that comes to mind and share their writing if they wish to do so. In this case, however, allow students as much time as they need to complete the activity.

Narrative Writing

Name _____ Date _____

Writing Narratives About Literature:
NARRATING PERSONAL CONNECTIONS

> A theme is an idea that can be stated in a sentence and suggests a universal truth that applies to many real-life situations. Books often have more than one theme.

A. Think of a theme in a book you know.

BOOK TITLE	A THEME IN THE BOOK

B. Now, quickly write about a personal experience you've had that's related to the theme.

_____

_____

_____

_____

_____

_____

100 Writing Lessons © by Tara McCarthy • Scholastic Teaching Resources

Narrative Writing

Writing About Literature: WIND-UP

Ask students to choose two pieces from their Writing Folders that they've written in this section to complete via the writing process. Provide a class period for start-up explorations with the two pieces; that is, students experiment with the two, then settle on one piece to develop, and attach a tag: "I'm choosing this piece to develop because . . . " (for example, ". . . it's almost finished"; ". . . it's more interesting"; ". . . it states my ideas very clearly.")

Have pupils polish their drafts, choose writing partners, and use the rubric on page 45 as a guideline in their conferences.

Narrative Writing

Name _____ Date _____

Writing About Literature: WIND-UP

After reading your partner's story, fill in the chart below. Then use the information as you confer with your partner about his or her story.

Your story helps me really understand . . .

	YES	NO	EXAMPLES
1. The story characters **2.** The story plot **3.** How the story is related to real life			

Narrative Writing

Writing Stories: INVESTIGATING PLOT IN TRADITIONAL STORIES

Goal: Review plot steps in traditional stories.

➡ Get Set

A familiar fairy tale, folktale, myth, or legend makes a good vehicle for quickly reviewing the components of a plot.

➡ Go

Draw a story-step graphic organizer like the reproducible on page 47 on the board, and choose a familiar traditional story to outline. Highlight the four elements in the reproducible. (Note: text in parentheses is the plot outline for "The Fox and the Grapes.")

3. Climax: The incident is the high point of a story in which the character either succeeds or fails in solving the problem. *(The fox sees that he can never get the grapes.)*

2. Complication: The incident tells how the main character tries to get what he or she wants. *(The fox jumps and jumps again in an attempt to get the grapes.)*

4. Resolution: The character faces the consequences of his or her actions or decisions. *(The fox decides that the grapes are probably sour anyway and not worth eating.)*

1. Conflict: The introduction shows an incident that tells who the main character is and what he or she wants. *(A hungry fox spies some grapes, but they're high above him on a vine.)*

➡ Follow Up

Work with the class or have partners or small groups work together to complete the reproducible for other familiar tales. Go over the broad criteria presented in the Tip below. Then have students adapt their story steps to modern times.

Tip Many students have a hard time initially discerning between complication and climax, or between climax and resolution. The main thing to look for in the story-steps graphic is motion: Does the action move along? Are the big events recorded? Does the last step show how the tale ends?

Narrative Writing

Name _____ Date _____

Writing Stories: INVESTIGATING PLOT IN TRADITIONAL STORIES

A. Record the plot of a fairy tale, folktale, myth, or legend in the story-step graphic organizer.

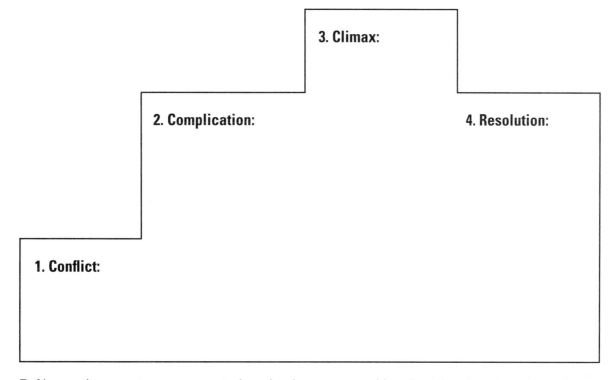

3. Climax:

2. Complication:

4. Resolution:

1. Conflict:

B. Now write a sentence or two to imagine how you would update the story to modern times. Here's an example for adapting "The Fox and the Grapes":

The fox wants a sandwich from a fast-food store, but he doesn't have any money.

_____

_____

_____

_____

_____

Narrative Writing

Writing Stories:
INVESTIGATING STORY CHARACTERS

> Goal: Focus on characters in a narrative.

➡ Get Set

Many young writers become very adept at settling on the bare bones of a story plot: this happened, then that happened, and then this is how it ended. The next thing these plot-savvy students want to learn is how to flesh out their skeleton narratives to make compelling stories, just as real authors do. The fleshing-out process starts by picturing characters before one begins to write.

➡ Go

On the board, draw a Venn diagram. Discuss the similarities and differences between key characters in a book that the class has recently read, and record students' responses in the Venn diagram. Then have students work in groups of five or six to talk about how the plot (conflict, complication, climax, resolution) grows out of these likenesses and differences. Here's an example for *My Brother Sam Is Dead:*

MAIN CHARACTERS IN <u>My Brother Sam Is Dead</u>

SAM
- quickly joins the American Revolution, defies his father
- will steal to achieve aims
- quickly takes risks
- never doubts the cause he's fighting for
- is executed by his own army

BOTH
- love their parents
- make hard decisions
- love one another
- suffer in the war

TIM
- follows his parents' loyalty to England
- supports his father
- disapproves of theft
- slowly learns to take risks
- often wonders whose side he's on
- lives to wonder and grieve

Bring the groups together to discuss their insights.

➡ Follow Up

Ask students to look through their Writing Folders for this narrative section to find two characters to describe in the Venn diagram on the page 49.

Tip Use the following as a discussion prompt: Imagine that the main characters feel exactly the same way and do exactly the same things. Would the plot be the same? Why not? How would the plot change?

Narrative Writing

Name _____ Date _____

Writing Stories:
INVESTIGATING STORY CHARACTERS

Look through the narratives you've written so far. Choose two characters to describe in the Venn diagram. Describe them as quickly as you can.

NOTE: This is not the final idea for a story. It's a fun activity to help you practice exploring the similarities and differences between characters.

MAIN CHARACTERS IN _____ **AND** _____

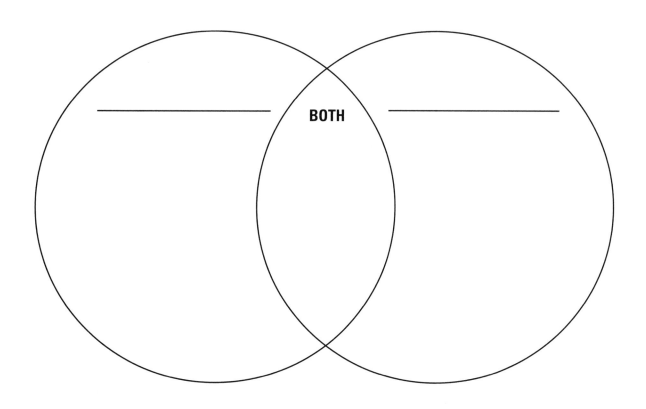

100 Writing Lessons © by Tara McCarthy • Scholastic Teaching Resources

Narrative Writing

Writing Stories: PICTURE THE SETTING

Goal: Visualize the place where a story happens.

➡Get Set

The setting of a story has a great deal to do with how characters behave and how they resolve their problems.

➡Go

Give small groups a reproduction of a landscape painting or photograph that is visually dramatic (e.g., deep canyons; rugged, snowy mountains; seascapes; aerial nighttime view of a city). Ask them to brainstorm for about five minutes some events that might happen in that setting. A group scribe can record ideas and then read them to the rest of the class as he or she displays the landscape.

➡Follow Up

Distribute the reproducible on page 51. Have students work independently to draw or paint a picture of the setting of a story they are planning to write. Remind them to include specific details. Then ask students to pencil in a sequence of story events and create a corresponding legend.

Tip By guiding students to plan the settings of their own realistic stories, you help them avoid incongruous time-events (such as a futuristic UFO rescuing a right-now cat from a tree) and place-events that jar the reader (such as a farm child leaving her rural home and immediately boarding a subway). Even fantasy stories are more convincing if students have spent some prewriting time thinking about time and place.

Narrative Writing

Name _____ Date _____

Writing Stories: PICTURE THE SETTING

A. Draw or paint a picture of the setting of a story you plan to write. Include specific details.

B. Now write in numerals to show the sequence of story events that might happen in this setting. Include a legend that briefly describes each event. (Example: 1. Ralph and his dog, Lucy, start here on the trail.) You can add more details to your picture at any point.

Narrative Writing

Narrative Writing

Writing Stories:
STORY PERKS AND STARTERS

Goal: Use group input to get stories going.

➡ Get Set

Students may drag their heels when it comes to the task of writing an original story for a number of reasons. They honestly may not have any story ideas, or they may be stopped by self-judgment: *My story has to be perfect from the very beginning.* Group writing activities provide the impetus that most hesitant students need to get moving. Keep these activities fun and fast!

➡ Go

Pass out a copy of the reproducible on page 53 to each student and divide the class into small groups. Go over each writing activity, modeling an example for each before assigning it.

Great Beginnings—Going On: Present exciting story openers and invite students to brainstorm a variety of things that might happen next. Have students continue the story on a separate sheet of paper.

Object Prompts: Prepare a large grab bag of 15–20 small items. Do this quickly and randomly. Tell each student to remove 2–4 items without looking and then, based on the items, immediately improvise a brief oral narrative of 3–4 sentences for the group. Ask other students to tell what they liked best about the mini-narrative.

Familiar Sayings: Discuss the familiar sayings and ask students to consider how rewording the sayings alters their meaning. Then have the group talk about situations in which a character discovers the truth of the saying.

New Endings for Old Stories—Going On: Share the traditional endings of familiar stories. Then suggest "just suppose" alternate endings and encourage students to brainstorm ways to continue the story.

➡ Follow Up

Ask each student to choose a story his or her group has discussed in one of the activities and list in sequence how the narrative might move along from start to finish. Then have them discuss the sequence with partners to see if it makes sense or if an event is missing.

Tip After each activity, offer this writing prompt: "If you wish, take some time now to make notes about how you might 'grow' your story."

Narrative Writing

Name _____ Date _____

Writing Stories:
STORY PERKS AND STARTERS

Great Beginnings—Going On

As the wind howled through the forest, Matt groped his way toward the flickering light in the distance. His foot struck a weird object and stumbled to the ground.

Warmth and peace! These are what the Earth Commanders felt when they landed on this distant planet, until they saw the tragic expressions of the beings who came to greet them.

Object Prompts

Objects: _____
_____
_____
_____

My Narrative: _____
_____
_____
_____
_____

Familiar Sayings

Saying	Rewording
Look before you leap.	
Haste makes waste.	
Many hands make light work.	
A friend in need is a friend indeed.	

New Endings for Old Stories—Going On

Ending	Alternate Ending	What Might Happen Next
The slipper fits, and Cinderella marries the prince. The fox can't reach the grapes.	The slipper fits, but Cinderella declines to marry the prince. The fox finally jumps up and gets the grapes.	

Narrative Writing

Writing Stories:
START YOUR STORY WITH A BANG!

> Goal: Provide a strategy for grabbing the audience's attention and helping the writer plunge into the story.

➡ Get Set

There are all sorts of exceptions, of course, but in a model story, the main character, the setting, and an interesting event are presented in the first sentence or paragraph. In writing narratives, as in writing plays, this is called setting the stage. When the stage is set compellingly, the audience wants to read on.

➡ Go

Distribute the reproducible on page 55. Talk about how the completed chart in section A combines character, setting, and an event. Point out how the information in the first row is used to create the first paragraph of a story. Focus on the idea that the paragraph focuses on a big event, presents the main character in action, leaves out minor details, and is exciting.

Ask students to work independently or with a partner to draft exciting story openers for the other information in the chart.

➡ Follow Up

Have students use what they've learned about narrative to write the opening paragraph of an original story.

Tip Introduce the Almost-Said strategy to students. The writer asks the audience: "What did I seem to be hinting at in my story opener? What would you like to know more about?" This strategy provides writers with new ideas and also serves as a checkpoint to inform them whether their story openers are engaging to their audience. Students may also use Mental Movies (page 24).

Narrative Writing

Name _____ Date _____

Writing Stories:
START YOUR STORY WITH A BANG!

A. This story opener chart combines character, setting, and an event.

MAIN CHARACTER	SETTING	FIRST MAIN EVENT
Megan: She is a foster child who feels unloved and unwanted.	An old house in the country, where Megan is living temporarily.	Megan sees a ghostly figure in the garden. The figure waves to her.
A Bear: He was born in the woods but has lost his way.	A shopping mall parking lot at night.	A shopper returns to her car and finds the bear sitting on it.
A Railroad Engineer: He's an old-timer who thinks he's seen everything.	A lonely stretch of track in the middle of nowhere.	A woman bursts into the engineer's cab and insists that he stop the train immediately.
A Clown: She is on her way to a circus in a distant city.	A plane having trouble in a thunderstorm.	Some fearful passengers begin to panic.

FIRST PARAGRAPH OF STORY:

Lonely and depressed, Megan Stuart kicked her way through the fields around the old house. She knew nobody wanted her. So who was that misty, cloudy figure waving to her from the garden in a such a friendly way?

B. Select one of the other story openers in the chart. On a separate sheet of paper, draft the first paragraph of a story that combines character, setting, and an exciting event.

Narrative Writing

Writing Stories: WIND-UP

Distribute the reproducible on page 57. Review with students the components of a good story that are summarized on the reproducible. Tell students to refer to the components as they draft, confer, and revise an original short story.

Suggest that as a prewriting strategy, students briefly discuss story plans with partners. After partners confer to determine if all the components appear in their drafts, each writer may want to ask for more specific feedback, as shown in the following examples:

- "I want to make (character's name) is really funny and likeable. Does this come across? Do you have any suggestions?"
- "Close your eyes as I read this section. Tell me what you see in your mind's eye."
- "Tell me what the strongest parts of my story are. What do you think makes them strong?"

Before students revise, remind them that many professional writers usually make several drafts of a story before they hammer out the final copy. While your students need not write a series of drafts, they should be allowed a couple of class periods to refine parts of their stories, perhaps testing out the refinements with their writing partners.

With the class, brainstorm publishing ideas such as the following:
- A class short-story anthology
- Individual books with covers and illustrations
- Dramatization of stories in a Readers Theater
- *A Writer's Best* newsletter for families and other classmates, in which each student selects for publication a story passage that he or she is particularly proud of
- Read-alouds to present in classrooms or the library
- An Author's Lunch where each writer speaks briefly about the problems he or she encountered in writing the story; the fun of story-writing; and the next stories he or she plans to write.

Narrative Writing

Name _____ Date _____

Writing Stories: WIND-UP

Keep the components of a good story in mind as you create your own original story.

COMPONENTS OF A GOOD STORY

1. Characters:

The main character has a problem to solve.

The characters are believable and interesting.

2. Plot:

The events are told in the order in which they happen.

All the important events are included.

The plot makes sense.

3. Setting:

It's clear to the reader where and when the story takes place.

4. Language:

The writer uses vivid, exact words.

---

100 Writing Lessons © by Tara McCarthy • Scholastic Teaching Resources

Narrative Writing

Name _____ Date _____

On Your Own:
IMAGINATION DIARIES

Imagine yourself in the future. What do you think you'll be like in 25 years? What will you be doing? Write a journal or diary entry describing a day in your future life.

100 Writing Lessons © by Tara McCarthy • Scholastic Teaching Resources

Name _____ Date _____

On Your Own:
IMAGINATION DIARIES

Write a newspaper article about a key historical event you've been studying. Send your imagination traveling back in time. Present the facts and details of this event as if it's hot news! Don't forget to include an eye-catching headline. For example, if you were studying ancient Egypt, you might create newspaper articles for headlines like these:

PHARAOH COMPLAINS ABOUT SLOW PACE OF PYRAMID CONSTRUCTION
NILE FLOODS RIGHT ON TIME!
NEFERTITI ASCENDS THRONE TO CHEERS

Ideas for Headlines:

Article:

Narrative Writing

Name _____ Date _____

On Your Own:
CHARACTER ADVERTISEMENTS

Choose a favorite character from a story and then write and illustrate an advertisement to convince other readers that they'll enjoy reading about the character, too. Post your ads on the class bulletin board.

100 Writing Lessons © by Tara McCarthy • Scholastic Teaching Resources

Narrative Writing

Name _____ Date _____

On Your Own:
TELL ME WHAT YOU SEE

Draw a picture of an event from your own life. Exchange your picture with a partner. Now write a short story based on what you see in the picture.

100 Writing Lessons © by Tara McCarthy • Scholastic Teaching Resources

Narrative Writing

Name _____ Date _____

On Your Own:
SOUNDTRACK

Movies and television shows have soundtracks: music that highlights the mood of the story. Think of one of your favorite songs or pieces of music. What story ideas come to you as you listen to the music? Does it suggest characters, setting, or events? What kind of mood does the music create?

Write a story that will have the music you selected as a soundtrack.

_____

_____

_____

_____

_____

_____

_____

_____

_____

_____

_____

_____

_____

_____

100 Writing Lessons © by Tara McCarthy • Scholastic Teaching Resources

Narrative Writing

Name _____ Date _____

On Your Own: RATE YOURSELF

1. For you, what's the most challenging or hardest thing about narrative writing?

_____

_____

_____

_____

2. For you, what's the easiest thing about narrative writing?

_____

_____

_____

_____

3. Of all the narrative writing you've done in this section, which piece pleases you the most? Why?

_____

_____

_____

_____

4. Of all the narrative writing you've done in this section, which pleases you the least? Why?

_____

_____

_____

_____

100 Writing Lessons © by Tara McCarthy • Scholastic Teaching Resources

Narrative Writing

Composition: PRECISE NOUNS

The difference between the noun *food* and words like *pizza, eggs, carrots, cupcake,* and *fishstick* demonstrates the importance of using precise nouns. Go over the definition of precise that appears at the top of the reproducible on page 65.

Write the following sentences and nouns on the board:

1. He faced a <u>lot of hard things</u> bravely.

2. We had an interesting <u>fight</u> about politics.

3. She stared in <u>surprise</u> at the Grand Canyon.

4. They found <u>little pieces of things</u> from the meteorite.

5. I've reached the <u>general idea</u> that writing can be fun.

> **awe**   **hardships**   **fragments**   **conclusion**   **argument**

Challenge students to find precise nouns in the box to replace the underlined noun or noun phrase in each sentence.

More Practice

Have students search through their Writing Folder to find a piece of writing that they could improve by making the nouns more precise. After they rewrite the piece, encourage students to share both the original and the rewrite with a partner.

100 Writing Lessons © by Tara McCarthy • Scholastic Teaching Resources

Name _____ Date _____

Composition: PRECISE NOUNS

Precise means accurate, exact. Think of a precise noun as a camera with an accurate, exact focus. The precise noun delivers a word-picture that shows the reader exactly what you mean. Without precise nouns, those word-pictures will be blurry and out of focus. Look at the examples below.

There was a lot of stuff on the shelves.　　　**There was a variety of toys on the shelves.**

Even when you think you're using precise nouns, you might be surprised to find that you can be even more specific. Even though two words may be synonyms, they might still have important differences in meaning.

Use a dictionary or thesaurus to find the important differences in meaning in each pair of nouns below. Then write sentences that show the difference in meaning precisely.

---

1. terror, panic　　**2.** secret, mystery　　**3.** promise, agreement

4. mixture, blend　　**5.** form, outline　　**6.** shock, amazement

---

Narrative Writing

Composition: STRONG VERBS

Start students on the road to incorporating strong verbs into their writing by copying the following sentences and box of verbs on the board:

1. She <u>looked</u> <u>angrily</u> at me.
2. The fire <u>made</u> <u>little</u> <u>noise</u>.
3. We <u>looked</u> <u>very</u> <u>closely</u> at the moth.
4. He <u>held</u> the bat <u>tightly</u>.
5. They <u>called</u> <u>very</u> <u>loudly</u>.
6. She <u>walked</u> <u>slowly</u> in the garden.

> **crackled   glared   gripped   strolled   hollered   studied**

Call on students to find a strong verb in the box to replace the underlined words in each sentence and rewrite it. Then distribute the reproducible on page 67 and go over it with students.

More Practice

Have students search through their Writing Folder to find a piece of writing that they could improve by making the verbs stronger. After they rewrite the piece, encourage students to share both the original and the rewrite with a partner.

Narrative Writing

Name _____ Date _____

Composition: STRONG VERBS

A strong verb is a verb with muscles. On its own, it can carry just as much or even more meaning than a string of weaker words.

Pretty weak!: The lights <u>shine off and on</u> in the distance as the little boat <u>moves from side to side</u> in the water.

Strong!: The lights <u>glimmer</u> in the distance as little boat <u>rocks</u> in the water.

Use a dictionary or thesaurus to find the important differences in meaning between each pair of verbs below. Then write a brief paragraph in which you use at least five of the verbs in the box.

1. bother, fluster	**3. swagger, prance**
2. coax, plead	**4. admire, appreciate**

Narrative Writing

Across the Curriculum:
WRITING ABOUT SOCIAL STUDIES

Writing about social studies topics can seem dry and boring to students if they think they have to stick to a bare-bones recital of facts. Narrative writing techniques can give readers a sense of "being there" when the Declaration of Liberty was signed, on an exploration of Mayan pyramids, or on the floor of the New York Stock Exchange.

Model how you might make a social studies topic more narrative:

The Draft:
The Mississippi River
The Mississippi River is 2,340 miles (3,770 kilometers) long. It starts in Minnesota and ends in Louisiana. It is the second longest river in the United States.
The Revision:
Two-Thousand-Three-Hundred-Thirty-Nine Miles to Go
On July 4, 2002, Martin Strel slipped into the waters of Lake Itasca, Minnesota. Lake Itasca is the source of the Mississippi River. Then Strel swam the entire length of the river—all 2,340 miles (or 3,770 kilometers) of it. The swim down the second-largest river in the United States took him 68 days! In early September, Strel reached Louisiana, where the river flows into the Gulf of Mexico.

With students, brainstorm a list of familiar social studies topics that could serve as the subject of a narrative paragraph, such as the founding of their community, how coins are made, the current U.S. president, the Boston Tea Party, and so on.

Write About Social Studies

Pair students, and pass out one copy of the reproducible on page 69 to each set of partners. Tell students that they'll be taking on the role of famous people with similar interests or achievements but who lived in different times. For instance, the 19th-century explorer Meriwether Lewis and the 20th-century astronaut Sally Ride might correspond with each other about the challenges of exploring.

Establish some simple criteria such as the following:
- Use the first-person point of view.
- Write about real events. Refer to textbooks and other print and Internet resources to find the facts.
- Use your imagination. Put yourself in the shoes of a historical figure. How do you think he or she responded to the events?

Narrative Writing

Name _____ Date _____

Across the Curriculum:
WRITING ABOUT SOCIAL STUDIES

Choose two historical figures who have something in common—BUT who lived in different time periods. What do you think they would say in their letters to each other ? What would they be curious to know about each other?

A. Take on the roles of the historical figures and write letters to each other.

_____

B. Now exchange letters. Write your response to the letter you received.

_____

Descriptive Writing

Exploring Sensory Imagery: DO YOU SEE WHAT I SEE?

Goal: Help students appreciate the uniqueness of their own "visual take."

➡ Get Set

Arm students with sketch pads and pencils and lead them on an observational field trip around the classroom, outside the school, or in the immediate neighborhood. Tell students to make quick sketches of at least four things that catch their eye. Suggest that eye-catchers may be underfoot (rugs, puddles, plants, bugs), at eye level (bulletin boards, playground equipment, vehicles, people, windows, doors), or high up (ceiling fans, cloud formations, birds in flight, tall buildings, planes).

➡ Go

On your return, discuss what students noticed on the field trip and list the items on the board. The list will probably be pretty general.

Then ask each student to choose his or her favorite sketch to describe. Hand out copies of the reproducible on page 72. Challenge students to be as descriptive—and brief—as possible in writing a label for their sketch. Remind them to sign their label.

Group the sketches in general categories, such as animals, buildings, and so on. For each category, briefly discuss with the class the similarities and differences in what caught the eye of each artist. Ask: *How does each picture in the category help you see something special about the subject?*

➡ Follow Up

Have students who pictured similar subjects work together to write a paragraph about their different views of the subject.

Tip Encourage students to carry small notebooks with them so they can record their observations wherever they are.

Descriptive Writing

100 Writing Lessons © by Tara McCarthy • Scholastic Teaching Resources

Name _____ Date _____

Exploring Sensory Imagery:
DO YOU SEE WHAT I SEE?

A. Choose your favorite sketch. Glue it or redraw it in the box below.

By: _____

B. Write a brief label for your sketch. What do you see? Be descriptive!

Descriptive Writing

Exploring Sensory Imagery:
SEEING DETAILS

> Goal: Focus students' attention on visual details.

➡ Get Set

Collect six ordinary objects that can be displayed on a table, such as a vase, a calendar, a lunchbox, a box of crayons, a book, a glove or mitten—and a sheet to cover the display.

Tell students that they will get several five-second glimpses of items on the table. Each time, they must follow the directions you give beforehand. (After each glimpse, cover the display with the sheet and give students time to record their responses. Uncover the display again to verify the responses. Then cover the display again to rearrange it.) Distribute copies of the reproducible on page 74.

➡ Go

Give students three five-second glimpses of the display.

- Glimpse 1: Display four items.
- Glimpse 2: Add the two other items.
- Glimpse 3: Remove one or two items.

➡ Follow Up

Vary, build, and improvise on the activity according to your students' abilities. For example, arrange items on the left, middle, and right; put some items under the table; shorten observation time to three or four seconds; or add a tag to one or more items and ask students to identify what's been added.

Tip If students are having trouble remembering all the items, suggest that they close their eyes and try to visualize what they saw on the table. They may remember more than they realize!

Descriptive Writing

Name _____ Date _____

Exploring Sensory Imagery: SEEING DETAILS

You have five seconds to look at each display of items. Write down what you see.

A. Glimpse 1: Name the items you saw.

_____

_____

_____

_____

Details I missed: _____

B. Glimpse 2: Name the items that were added.

_____

_____

_____

_____

Details I missed: _____

C. Glimpse 3: Name the items that were taken away.

_____

_____

_____

_____

Details I missed: _____

100 Writing Lessons © by Tara McCarthy • Scholastic Teaching Resources

Descriptive Writing

Exploring Sensory Imagery:
REMEMBERING VISUAL DETAILS

Goal: Further sharpen students' attention to visual details.

➡ Get Set

Select a poster or a photo to display on the overhead projector that has several major features, such as people, action, landscape details, colors, or shapes. Explain to students that they'll have about 30 seconds to examine the visual and then list from memory as many details from it as possible on the reproducible on page 76.

➡ Go

After displaying the visual, allow students about four minutes to list the details they saw. Then have small groups compare their lists and compile a group master list to share with the rest of the class. Show the visual again and encourage students to discuss the accuracy and completeness of their lists.

➡ Follow Up

Ask each student to write a paragraph describing the scene in the picture. For vivid results, encourage the use of present-tense verbs.

Tip Point out real-life occasions when we get just a quick look at something that we wish we had more time to study: when we travel in a car, bus, train, or plane; when something moves quickly past us as we stand still: a bird in flight, a fire truck, a parade. Discuss why "Look close, look fast/it may not last!" is a good slogan for writers to remember.

Descriptive Writing

Name _____ Date _____

Exploring Sensory Imagery:
REMEMBERING VISUAL DETAILS

A. Write down what you saw in the visual. Record as many details as you can.

My List
_____
_____
_____
_____
_____

B. Compare your list with the other lists your group made.

C. Combine your lists to create one group list.

Our List
_____
_____
_____
_____
_____

D. Share your list with the other groups in class.

100 Writing Lessons © by Tara McCarthy • Scholastic Teaching Resources

Descriptive Writing

Exploring Sensory Imagery:
IT'S IN THE BAG

Goal: Describe ordinary objects accurately, without seeing them.

➡ Get Set

In a laundry bag, place four or five items that share some similar features such as shape, size, or texture—and perhaps some similarities in use as well—such as the following:

- mallet, hammer, gavel, drumstick
- tweezers, pliers, kitchen tongs, hairpin
- lipstick, glue stick, crayon, pencil
- apple, pear, grape, orange, onion
- baseball, tennis ball, ping-pong ball, football

Model the activity for students. Reach into the laundry bag and choose an object, without looking. Identify it through touch and then describe it to students, without naming it or the specific task for which it's used: *This object is about eight inches long. It has two hands or arms on it, which you squeeze together to pull out things. The object is made of metal, and this one has rubber tips at the ends of the hands or arms.* (pliers)

➡ Go

Ask students to draw the object based on your description. After revealing the object, ask: *Which of my words and phrases helped you form a picture of the object in your mind's eye? What details could I have added?* List their responses on the board. Then pair students and have them repeat the activity, taking turns describing and drawing items in the bag.

➡ Follow Up

Ask students to refer to their reproducibles (page 78) as they independently write a paragraph that compares and contrasts two of the objects.

Tip Emphasize the skills involved in the activity:
- A really super describer will give such thorough clues about shape, size, texture (and maybe even color) that the listener will be able to draw the object without hearing its name.
- A really super listener will be so attentive to the descriptive details that he or she will be able to draw the object being described.

Descriptive Writing

100 Writing Lessons © by Tara McCarthy • Scholastic Teaching Resources

Name _____ Date _____

Exploring Sensory Imagery:
IT'S IN THE BAG

Listen to the description of the object. Write down the descriptive words and phrases. Then use the descriptions to identify and draw the object.

Descriptive Words and Phrases	Object

Descriptive Writing

Exploring Sensory Imagery:
JUST LOOK AT THOSE
SMELLS AND TASTES!

Goal: Link smells and tastes to senses of touch, sight, and hearing.

➡ Get Set

A way to describe tastes and smells is by linking them to our other senses: *The peppery stew nearly blinded me.* (taste: sight) *Her perfume shouted for attention.* (smell: hearing) Blending senses like this is called synesthesia.

➡ Go

For this activity, you'll need a color chart or a spectrum chart. In a quick-go-round, indicate a color on the chart and call on two or three volunteers to tell what taste or smell the color brings to mind. The faster the response, the better—and almost anything goes!

Display a copy of the reproducible on page 80 on an overhead or create a similar chart on the board. Record the volunteers' responses.

➡ Follow Up

Invite students to choose a color and write a poem or paragraph that tells what the color brings to mind in terms of tastes and smells (and in terms of sounds and touch as well, if they'd like).

Tip You may need to prime the pump with some examples linking color with taste and smell and translating the example into a phrase:
- When I see this color, red, I think of the smell of roses. (the red smell of roses)
- This color, gray, reminds me of the taste of cold oatmeal. (a gray taste, like cold oatmeal)
- To me, this shade of pale green is like the taste of ocean water. (the pale green taste of salty ocean water)
- The color pink smells to me like a field of wildflowers. (the smell of wildflowers drifted toward me like a pink cloud)

Descriptive Writing

Name _____ Date _____

Exploring Sensory Imagery:
JUST LOOK AT THOSE
SMELLS AND TASTES!

Your teacher will show you a color. What taste or smell does that color bring to mind? Record your responses in the chart.

Color	Taste of	Smell of

Descriptive Writing

Exploring Sensory Imagery: WHAT ARE THE WORDS FOR WHAT I HEAR?

Goal: Describe sounds with precision.

➡ Get Set

Most people have little difficulty identifying the sources of sounds such as a motorcycle or the sigh of someone who feels sad or frustrated. The trick is to build a vocabulary for precisely describing sounds and the actions that go with them.

➡ Go

Distribute the reproducible on page 82. Discuss how the lists are organized, and how writers can use them to expand their vocabulary. Provide examples such as the following:

- Ducklings *splashed* in the puddles.
- She *flopped* into the chair.
- He *thudded* along angrily.
- Skateboards *clattered* on sidewalks.

➡ Follow Up

Have students work independently or with a partner on the writing assignment described on the reproducible.

Tip Tape-record students as they read their paragraph to classmates. They can listen to the tapes later for review, to get story ideas, or just for fun.

Descriptive Writing

Name _____ Date _____

Exploring Sensory Imagery:
WHAT ARE THE WORDS FOR WHAT I HEAR?

Fast, Light Sounds and Actions

scamper, skitter, scoot, slide, slip, slither, slink, sled, slice

Unhappy, Angry Sounds and Actions

moan, groan; growl, grump, grouse
snarl, snort, snicker; wail, whine, whimper

Deep Sounds and Heavy Actions

thump, thunder, thud; rumble, grumble, mumble, tumble

Blowing Sounds and Actions

blab, blubber, blow, blast, bubble, bluster, burble

Awkward Sounds and Actions

flubber, flounder, flop, flip, flump, flurry, fling

Sounds of Things Breaking

smash, crash, splash, dash
clatter, shatter

Sounds and Actions That End Fast

clip, snip; rap, tap, snap
crack, smack, thwack

Repeated Sounds and Actions

bow-wow, tick-tock, ding-dong, pitter-patter

A. Choose one of the lists above. Write a paragraph using at least four of the words in that list to describe an event filled with sound and action.

_____

_____

_____

_____

_____

_____

B. Alone or with a partner, revise and proofread your paragraph. Then read it aloud to some classmates. Ask your audience to listen for the sound-action words.

Descriptive Writing

Exploring Sensory Imagery: ALLITERATION

Goal: Increase use of alliteration in descriptive writing.

➡ Get Set

Alliteration is the use of initial consonant sounds in words that occur close together:
The fire flamed, and the coals crackled.

➡ Go

Read aloud the following examples of alliteration and ask students to listen for the repeated initial sounds:

- The bees were busy, feasting on fragrant flowers.
- Down in the dungeon, the prisoner paced and plotted.
- The kitten cringed, then darted toward the dish.
- The land lay low beneath the ridge, and rivers rippled through it.

After students identify each alliteration, write the example on the board.

➡ Follow Up

Distribute the reproducible on page 84 and discuss the alliteration cluster example. Assign a consonant sound to each student. Ask him or her to complete the alliteration cluster on the reproducible for that sound. Set aside time for students to share their work.

Tip Have students work in groups of four or five to look through poetry anthologies and chapter books to find phrases or sentences that contain alliteration. Ask groups to read some examples to the class.

Descriptive Writing

Name _____ Date _____

Exploring Sensory Imagery: ALLITERATION

A. Study and discuss these alliteration clusters.

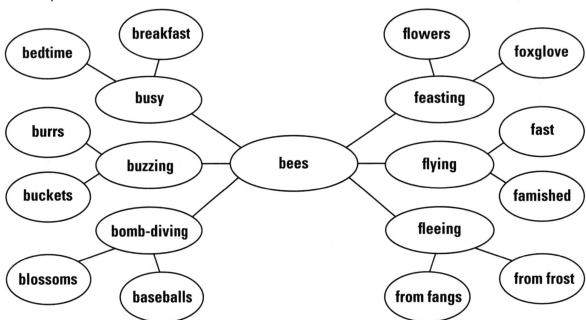

B. Now create your own alliteration clusters.

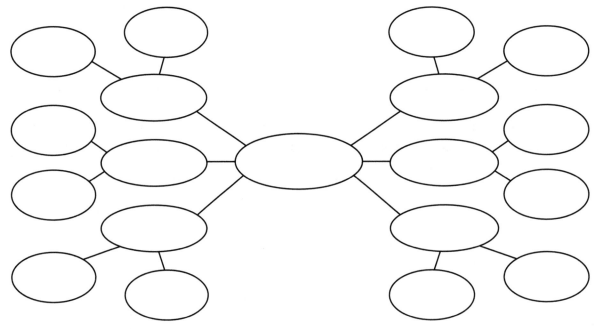

100 Writing Lessons © by Tara McCarthy • Scholastic Teaching Resources

Descriptive Writing

Exploring Sensory Imagery: WIND-UP

To review how writers use sensory images in descriptive writing, display a chart with categories of adjectives, nouns, and verbs.

sullen	girl	crept	bright	cold	room
frightened	cat	climbed	empty	warm	building
cautious	detective	peered	clammy	disorderly	office
unhappy	boy	fled	dark	musty	house
courageous	doctor	strolled	tremendous	ancient	forest

Model how you would create the beginning of a story by choosing a word from each column: *The courageous girl crept into the dark and ancient forest.*

Distribute the reproducible on page 86. Ask students to use the words in the chart to create three story beginnings.

Descriptive Writing

Name_____ Date _____

Exploring Sensory Imagery: WIND-UP

A. Choose an item from each column to create three different descriptive beginnings for stories. Write your beginnings on the lines below the chart.

sullen	girl	crept	bright	cold	room
frightened	cat	climbed	empty	warm	building
cautious	detective	peered	clammy	disorderly	office
unhappy	boy	fled	dark	musty	house
courageous	doctor	strolled	tremendous	ancient	forest

1. _____

_____

_____

_____

2. _____

_____

_____

_____

3. _____

_____

_____

_____

B. Choose one of your story beginnings. On the other side of this page, add to your story or write some ideas for ways to develop it.

100 Writing Lessons © by Tara McCarthy • Scholastic Teaching Resources

Descriptive Writing

Choosing Words That Work:
CLEANING OUT THE WORD CLOSET

Goal: Recognize and replace tired or trendy expressions with more effective ones.

➡ Get Set

In conversation, we all use worn-out words and stale clichés from time to time. But it's the trendy words and short-lived expressions that seem to be on every student's lips.

➡ Go

Copy the chart below on the board. After students read aloud the lists, ask if they can figure out why the columns are headed as they are. Help students notice that the words in the first column, opinion words, simply tell what someone thinks about a subject, while the words in the second column, fact words, show by supplying examples or sensory details.

OPINION WORDS	FACT WORDS
ugly	misshapen, splotchy
yukky	gooey, sweaty
awesome	snow-covered, steep
awful	shrill, tuneless
great	inspiring, rewarding
funny	humorous, unusual
nice	helpful, considerate
boring	slow-moving, repetitive

Encourage students to build the lists on the reproducible on page 88. Literature is the best source for adding to the Fact Words list. Ask students to listen for and note opinion words outside of school (TV ads and talk shows are excellent sources!) to add to the Opinion Words list.

➡ Follow Up

Have students make greeting cards with messages that *do not* use opinion words or tired expressions.

Tip Discuss the fact that we can often ask a *speaker* to clarify and give details, but we cannot just ask a *writer* for clarification. This is why writers try to supply readers with the necessary facts and imagery to grasp an idea or a scene clearly.

Descriptive Writing

Descriptive Writing

Name _____ Date _____

Choosing Words That Work:
CLEANING OUT THE WORD CLOSET

OPINION WORDS	FACT WORDS
ugly	misshapen, splotchy
yucky	gooey, sweaty
awesome	snow-covered, steep
awful	shrill, tuneless
great	inspiring, rewarding
funny	humorous, unusual
nice	helpful, considerate
boring	slow-moving, repetitive

Choosing Words That Work:
DEVELOPING CONTRASTS
WITH ANTONYMS

Goal: Build vocabulary for describing both subtle and strong differences.

➡ Get Set

Write the following sentence pairs on the board:

- The *glaring* lights *hit* us.
  The *soft* lights *caressed* us.
- The waves *surged* toward the *sunlit* beach.
  The waves *crept* toward the *dark* beach.
- Stunted trees *drooped* along the *narrow* path.
  Enormous trees *stretched* along the *wide* path.

Read aloud each sentence pair—without stressing the italicized antonyms. Have students close their eyes and listen to determine which words in the pair change the imagery.

➡ Go

After students identify the words in each pair, write the antonyms in columns on the board and discuss them.

Then distribute the reproducible on page 90, and discuss how the antonyms list can help students in their descriptive writing.

➡ Follow Up

Ask students to write a personality sketch of two television characters from the same or different sitcoms who are opposite from one another. Stress that the sketches should include many words and phrases that contrast the characters' appearances, personalities, and typical behavior, and that the sketches should not merely summarize plots or events.

Tip If necessary, define *antonyms* as words that have opposite or almost opposite meanings. You may wish to call out common words such as *big, slow, happy, heavy,* and *ugly* and have students supply antonyms.

Descriptive Writing

100 Writing Lessons © by Tara McCarthy • Scholastic Teaching Resources

Name_____ Date _____

Choosing Words That Work:
DEVELOPING CONTRASTS
WITH ANTONYMS

A. Use this antonym list as you do your descriptive writing.

round, circular ⟶	flat, level, straight
mute, silent, soundless ⟶	roaring, blasting, clattering
glance, peek, glimpse ⟶	stare, gape, gaze
sweet, fragrant, spicy ⟶	fetid, reeking, putrid
rough, coarse, scratchy ⟶	soft, silky, smooth
hurt, ache, painful ⟶	painless, pleasant, comfortable
brilliant, intelligent, wise ⟶	witless, dense, shortsighted
gullible, trusting ⟶	doubtful, mistrusting, skeptical
hazy, fuzzy, faint ⟶	distinct, clear, visible
tasty, flavorful, appetizing ⟶	bitter, offensive, sour
blazing, burning, fiery ⟶	cool, icy, chilly
solid, thick, dense ⟶	light, delicate, feathery

B. Add your own antonyms below.

Descriptive Writing

Choosing Words That Work:
CHOOSING AMONG SYNONYMS

> Goal: Develop a strategy for selecting the most precise descriptive word.

➡ Get Set

Discuss that synonyms are words with *almost* the same meaning, and that writers choose synonyms according to the context of a sentence. Display the reproducible on page 92 and present some examples—*bright* lights, *luminous* water, *radiant* sunshine, *gleaming* stars, *glossy* hair, *dazzling* smile.

➡ Go

Write sentences such as the following on the board. Distribute the reproducible on page 92. Tell students to read the sentences silently and then find a synonym on the reproducible that is more precise than the underlined word or phrase.

- She whistled a <u>happy</u> tune.
- My coat was <u>really wet</u>.
- The diamond ring looks <u>great</u>!

- He gave his report card a <u>sad</u> look.
- I could <u>eat</u> that sandwich in about two seconds!
- They stared at the creature in <u>a scared way</u>.

Call on students to share their revisions.

➡ Follow Up

Ask students to write a two-paragraph Personal Sketch about two incidents in their life that filled them with two different emotions or to which they reacted differently. Remind writers to use precise words that will help their readers visualize the experiences and understand how they were different.

> **Tip** Point out that the words grouped in each column of the antonym reproducible on page 90 are also synonyms—for example, *mute, silent, soundless; doubtful, mistrusting, skeptical.*

Descriptive Writing

Name_____ Date _____

Choosing Words That Work:
CHOOSING AMONG SYNONYMS

Use this list of synonyms and add to it as you do your descriptive writing.

Avoiding Things ————————➔ dodge, duck, shun, swerve, flee, escape

_____

Perfect ————————➔ flawless, complete, pure, spotless, fresh

_____

Shy ————————➔ modest, meek, humble, reserved, timid, coy

_____

Vain ————————➔ conceited, arrogant, proud, egotistical

_____

Cheerful ————————➔ merry, elated, lively, lighthearted, chipper

_____

Generous ————————➔ unselfish, big-hearted, liberal, lavish

_____

Impulsive ————————➔ hasty, careless, offhand, hurried, thoughtless

_____

Moist ————————➔ damp, soggy, soaking, drenched, saturated

_____

Eating ————————➔ devour, gobble, sip, taste, feast, chew

_____

Fear ————————➔ alarm, terror, dismay, dread, horror, anxiety

_____

Bright ————————➔ luminous, radiant, gleaming, glossy, dazzling

_____

Gloomy ————————➔ dreary, shady, dismal, somber, bleak, desolate

_____

Descriptive Writing

Choosing Words That Work: METAPHOR

> Goal: Use metaphor to build images and word pictures.

➡ Get Set

Write the following lines on the board:

- Wind is a cat/That prowls at night . . .
- All the world's a stage/And all the men and women merely players . . .
- You are my sunshine/My only sunshine . . .

Discuss the images with students and ask them what makes all the examples alike. (They compare one thing with another.) Review the term *metaphor:* a figure of speech that compares one thing with another.

➡ Go

Play a fast round of "Compare." Pass out the reproducible on page 94. Call on students to quickly come up with a metaphor that compares the pairs of words in the box. Model an example: moon – wheel: The moon was a bright wheel in the midnight sky.

Then have students choose one word pair to create a new metaphor and illustrate it on the reproducible.

➡ Follow Up

Have small groups look through books and anthologies to find at least five different examples of metaphor and then write each metaphor on a separate sheet of paper and illustrate it.

Tip You may want to introduce *metaphor*, *simile*, and *personification* by sharing the old saying, "Poets lie in order to tell the truth" with students. Poets make comparisons that, while not factually true, help readers experience the world in a new way.

Descriptive Writing

Name_____ Date _____

Choosing Words That Work: METAPHOR

A. Write a metaphor to compare a word pair in the box.

- truck – lion
- bed – ship
- window – eye
- cloud – pillow
- snow – feather
- lake – mirror

Word pair: _____ **Metaphor:** _____

B. Illustrate your metaphor.

My Metaphor: _____

Descriptive Writing

Choosing Words That Work: SIMILE

> Goal: Use similes to build images and word pictures.

➡ Get Set

Write the following lines by the poet Carl Sandburg on the board:

Life is like an onion: You peel it off one layer at a time and sometimes you weep.

Discuss the image with students and ask how it is similar to and different from a metaphor. (Similar: It compares one thing with another; Different: It uses the words *as* or *like*.) Review the term *simile:* a figure of speech that uses *as* or *like* to compare one thing with another.

➡ Go

Play a fast round of "Compare." Pass out the reproducible on page 96. Call on students to quickly come up with a simile that compares the pairs of words in the box. Model an example: moon – wheel: The moon was like a bright wheel in the midnight sky.

Then have students choose one word pair to create a new simile and illustrate it on the reproducible.

➡ Follow Up

Have small groups look through books and anthologies to find at least five different examples of similes and then write each on a separate sheet of paper and illustrate it.

Tip Encourage students to use similes and metaphors and other sensory language in the factual reports they're writing for science and social studies. Explain that such descriptive language can help readers get a better sense of natural phenomena or historical events.

Descriptive Writing

100 Writing Lessons © by Tara McCarthy • Scholastic Teaching Resources

Name _____ Date _____

Choosing Words That Work: SIMILE

A. Write a simile to compare a word pair in the box.

> • leaf – page   • smile – sun   • road – ribbon
> • hair – waterfall   • music – laughter   • sadness – gray

Word pair: _____ **Simile:** _____

B. Illustrate your simile.

My Simile: _____

Descriptive Writing

Choosing Words That Work:
PERSONIFICATION

> **Goal:** Become adept at using personification in writing.

➡ Get Set

Personification is a metaphor in which human characteristics are ascribed to nonhuman things. (The sun smiles down on us. The thunder threatens us. The stars wink.)

➡ Go

Write this poem on the board.

> The hail falls pitterpat,
> And fiercely rattles down upon
> The brave old pine tree's hat
> —Basho

Explain the term personification and discuss the images in the poem with students. To what is the pine tree being compared? (a brave old man or woman wearing a hat). Challenge pairs or small groups to find examples of personification in literature that the class has been studying.

➡ Follow Up

Have students use the reproducible on page 98 as the basis for a piece of writing on personification.

> **Tip** Point out that the image comparing the wind to a cat on page 93 is an example of personification.

Descriptive Writing

Name _____ Date _____

Choosing Words That Work:
PERSONIFICATION

A. Choose a nonhuman entity from the box.

- a tired pencil
- the family car
- a mosquito
- the chalkboard
- the school hallway
- a deserted house
- a hurricane
- a student's desk
- the playground at recess
- a lost sock
- a frog
- a sandwich

B. Write a poem, journal entry, or anecdote from that entity's "I" point of view.

_____

_____

_____

_____

_____

_____

_____

_____

_____

_____

_____

_____

_____

Descriptive Writing

Choosing Words That Work: WIND-UP

Ask students to imagine that they are their favorite book. Using their descriptive skills—especially personification—they write about what the book senses and feels about the story between its covers.

Being a Book

Write the title of your favorite book, and then "speak" for it. Complete the sentences to tell readers what they can expect.

My name is _____
　　　　　　　(title of book)

1. Here are some of the sounds you'll hear between my covers:

_____

_____

_____

2. I'm full of images. You'll probably like the sight of

_____

_____

_____But the image of_____

_____

_____may make you feel anxious, sad, or angry.

3. Turn my pages, and get ready to taste _____

_____ , touch _____

_____ , and smell _____

_____

4. The characters who live inside me experience many different feelings.

For example, _____feels_____
　　　　　(name of character)

when _____

_____

5. I highly recommend myself to you, because _____

_____

Model how you would fill out one of the sections for the title you've chosen. Distribute the reproducible on page 100 and have students complete it to bring the book of their choice to life.

Descriptive Writing

Name _____ Date _____

Choosing Words That Work: WIND-UP

Being a Book

Write the title of your favorite book, and then "speak" for it. Complete the sentences to tell readers what they can expect.

My name is _____

(title of book)

1. Here are some of the sounds you'll hear between my covers:

_____

_____

_____

2. I'm full of images. You'll probably like the sight of _____

_____

_____

_____ But the image of _____

_____

_____ may make you feel anxious, sad, or angry.

3. Turn my pages, and get ready to taste _____

_____ , touch _____

_____ , and smell _____

_____

4. The characters who live inside me experience many different feelings.

For example, _____ feels _____

(name of character)

when _____

_____

5. I highly recommend myself to you, because _____

_____

100 Writing Lessons © by Tara McCarthy • Scholastic Teaching Resources

Descriptive Writing

Organizing Descriptive Paragraphs:
TOP TO BOTTOM, SIDE TO SIDE

Goal: Introduce spatial organization in descriptive writing.

➡ Get Set

Show a household object such as a broom, lamp, small radio, or basket with a handle. Ask students to imagine that they are seeing the object for the first time and—as careful reporters—they are describing it to an intrigued audience of listeners or readers. The object should be described from top to bottom or from side to side.

➡ Go

Model an example, stressing position words as you point out the object's features (in this case, a broom held with the bristles on top): *This peculiar item is about five feet tall. At the top are hundreds of long bristles, bound about midway with cord. Below the binding, the bristles are attached to a long wooden pole about two inches in diameter. At the bottom of the pole is a small metal ring.*

Reverse the position of the broom (bristles at the bottom) and call on a volunteer to describe it in this position. Continue to work with students to describe another object from left to right or right to left, again stressing position words (*right, left, middle, center, beside, next to,* and so on).

➡ Follow Up

Distribute the reproducible on page 102 and preview the lists. Ask partners to refer to and use the lists as they draft a description of an ordinary classroom object. The challenge is for them to describe the object so well that classmates will be able to identify it. After students read aloud their description, ask the audience which detail and position words helped them identify the object.

Tip Use the image of a time capsule to introduce the lesson. Discuss with students that the things people store in time capsules are often objects that seem quite ordinary, but might be puzzling and intriguing to people opening the capsules a century or more from now.

Descriptive Writing

100 Writing Lessons © by Tara McCarthy • Scholastic Teaching Resources

Name_____ Date _____

Organizing Descriptive Paragraphs:
TOP TO BOTTOM, SIDE TO SIDE

POSITION WORDS
TOP TO BOTTOM, BOTTOM TO TOP, SIDE TO SIDE

above	below	inside
across from	beneath	leading to
against	beside	middle
along the side of	close to	near
at the base of	down	next to
at the bottom of	halfway	top
at the left	in back of	under, underneath
at the right	over	up
behind	in front of	upon

Use the list of position words as you and a partner draft a description of an ordinary object in the classroom *without* revealing the name of the object in your writing. Then read aloud your description and see if your classmates can guess what it is.

Descriptive Writing

Organizing Descriptive Paragraphs:
NEAR TO FAR, FAR TO NEAR

Goal: Choose a focal point and then move away from it or toward it.

➡ Get Set

Briefly discuss how choosing a visual focus for a description can help the audience see a scene or event clearly. Ask students to close their eyes to prepare for a visual trip and explain that you will describe a scene.

➡ Go

Read aloud the following description, stressing the underlined words:

Around you, snow-covered trees hang down over the path. A few steps underline{ahead} is an icy stream, flowing underline{away from} you, curling toward the tiny cabin underline{in the distance}. Beyond the cabin, hills loom up, their peaks seeming to disappear into the underline{faraway} clouds.

Question students as to whether the description takes them from upclose to farther away, or from far away to upclose (near to far).

Explain to students that on this far-to-near visual trip, they are to listen for spatial words and phrases, and also be able to name the object being described (fire engine): *The red speck underline{on the horizon} gets larger as it moves underline{toward} me. Hurrying forward past the park, it clangs and whines with a underline{growing} clamor. Now it is underline{halfway} up the block, now it is underline{next to} me for a moment, passing underline{close} enough to deafen me with its noise.* Distribute the reproducible on page 104. Have students complete the activity individually or with a partner.

➡ Follow Up

Tell students to write a story-opener paragraph that describes the story setting. Suggest the following settings: a forest, a deserted building, a shopping mall, a mountain top. Have them imagine they are in this setting and then choose a focus—near to far or far to near—and stick to it.

Tip One way for partners to start the conference stage for their story openers is to employ the visual-trip technique. As the writer reads the paragraph aloud, the partner listens to the description with eyes closed, then comments on what he or she saw while listening.

Descriptive Writing

Name _____ Date _____

Organizing Descriptive Paragraphs: NEAR TO FAR, FAR TO NEAR

POSITION WORDS
NEAR TO FAR, FAR TO NEAR

above	behind	inside
ahead	beside	midway
around	beyond	near
at a distance	close	next to
away from	faraway	outside
behind	forward	top
beneath	halfway	toward

Select a focus—near to far or far to near—and then revise the paragraph below to make the focus clear. Use the list of position words to help you describe the setting.

This street changes as you walk along it. Next to my house is an empty lot filled with strong, scraggly weeds and wildflowers. In the distance, I can see two towering office buildings. Just beyond the lot is Mrs. Jimez's news shop. Coming out of my front door, I walk through my mother's sunny flower garden. As I pass the shop, rows of apartments line the street.

_____

_____

_____

_____

_____

_____

Descriptive Writing

Organizing Descriptive Paragraphs: ORGANIZING WITH TIME-ORDER WORDS

Goal: Practice using time-order words in describing a series of actions.

➡ Get Set

Write the following paragraph on the board, providing blanks as shown.

___(As)___ I waded through the knee-high grass, I saw a hawk circling above. ___(For a moment)___ , it disappeared behind a distant clump of trees, ___(then)___ swerved upward again like a kite that had broken free of its string. ___(Just as)___ I was marveling at its flight, the hawk plunged to the ground and captured a field mouse. I ___(last)___ caught sight of the great bird as it arched upward ___(until)___ it was only a sunny flash against the crystal-blue air.

➡ Go

Distribute the reproducible on page 106. Ask students to select words from the list on the reproducible to fill in the blanks on the board and make the sequence of events in the paragraph clearer. Record their responses in the blanks. (Examples are given above.) Then have students complete the assignment on the reproducible.

➡ Follow Up

Suggest that students review the story-setting paragraph they wrote for page 103 and continue with another paragraph that tells about an event or series of actions that takes place in that setting, using time-order words to make the sequence clear.

Tip To review visual focus, ask students the following questions about the paragraph: Where is the narrator standing? (in a field) What is the general focus? (up and down).

Descriptive Writing

Name _____ Date _____

Organizing Descriptive Paragraphs:
ORGANIZING WITH
TIME-ORDER WORDS

TIME-ORDER WORDS

after	finally	later
afterward	first	meanwhile
as	for a moment	next
at the same time	immediately	soon
before	instantly	then
before long	just as	until
earlier	last	

Work with a partner to write a paragraph about an exciting event, real or fictional. Use one of the titles below or think of a title and an idea of your own. Follow these guidelines:

- Use time-order words to help readers follow the action.
- Use sensory words and metaphors to help readers follow the action.
- Do not write a paragraph about a dream!

Titles and Ideas

- Emergency Landing
- The Bear in the Tree
- A Noise in the Basement
- Lost on the Fairgrounds
- The Wrong Shoe
- The Terrible Picnic
- Big Storm
- The Happiest Day
- Where's the Cat?

_____

_____

_____

_____

_____

Descriptive Writing

Organizing Descriptive Paragraphs:
DESCRIBING PEOPLE

> Goal: Focus on a particular quality of an individual and organize a description around that focus.

➡ Get Set

On the board, list eight or ten characters from books and stories that your students have read. Include outstanding minor characters as well as major ones and villains as well as heroes.

➡ Go

Challenge students to come up with one descriptive word or phrase that sums up a major quality of each character. Chart students' ideas. Keep the activity moving fast—first reactions are the most powerful.

CHARACTER	MAJOR QUALITY
Matt (*My Brother Sam Is Dead*)	confused
Gretel ("Hansel and Gretel")	clever
Roderick Usher ("The Fall of the House of Usher")	depressed and secretive

Distribute the reproducible on page 108. Have students copy the chart on the reproducible. Ask the class to choose one of the characters and develop a descriptive paragraph that *shows* the character *acting* in a typical way.

➡ Follow Up

For the Follow Ups on pages 103 and 105, students create a paragraph that describes a story setting and a paragraph that describes a series of actions. Ask them to read over these paragraphs and then add a third one. It should describe a character by showing—not telling about—one of his or her major characteristics.

Tip Talk with students about their options for the third paragraph: The paragraph need not be related at all to the first two; however, many students will want to tie it in, because they sense a short story developing.

Descriptive Writing

Name_____ Date _____

100 Writing Lessons © by Tara McCarthy • Scholastic Teaching Resources

Organizing Descriptive Paragraphs:
DESCRIBING PEOPLE

CHARACTER	MAJOR QUALITY
_____	_____
_____	_____
_____	_____
_____	_____

Choose one of the characters in the chart above and develop a descriptive paragraph that *shows* the character *acting* in a typical way. You may also add a character and his or her major quality to the chart to write about.

_____
_____
_____
_____
_____
_____
_____
_____
_____
_____
_____
_____

Descriptive Writing

Organizing Descriptive Paragraphs:
ORGANIZING PARAGRAPHS
OF CONVERSATION

> Goal: Practice incorporating descriptive techniques when writing dialogue.

➡ Get Set

Copy the following chart onto the board. Leave the last column blank.

SETTING	SITUATION	CHARACTERS & QUALITIES	WHAT THEY DO: *ACTION*	WHAT THEY SAY: *DIALOGUE*
Playground	School bully approaches Lena and Hester at lunch	**Billy:** bully, mean and full of himself **Lena:** shy, scared **Hester:** protective, brave	Demands Lena's lunch Gives up lunch Grabs lunch back	("Gimme that, you squirt!) (Says nothing) ("Leave her alone! Get out of here!")

➡ Go

Ask students to brainstorm some dialogue the different characters in the chart might say, giving consideration to the situation presented and the characters' personalities. Enter students' ideas in the last column and punctuate contributions as dialogue. (Examples are shown in parentheses.)

Distribute the reproducible on page 110. Have students work independently or with a partner to use the chart to plan a story opener.

➡ Follow Up

Challenge students to add a fourth paragraph to the story they've been developing in the Follow Up activities on pages 103, 105, and 107. Suggest they add a second character who has different qualities than the main character or narrator, and create a dialogue between them.

> **Tip** Suggest that students read aloud their fourth paragraphs with a partner to see whether the dialogue sounds natural. Does the dialogue show two different people reacting in two quite different ways?

Name _____ Date _____

Organizing Descriptive Paragraphs: ORGANIZING PARAGRAPHS OF CONVERSATION

Use the chart below to plan a story opener.

Setting of My Story:

_____

_____

_____

_____

Here's the situation as the story opens:

Characters' Names and What They're Like	What the Characters Do: ACTION	What the Characters Say: DIALOGUE
1.		
2.		
3.		

Descriptive Writing

Organizing Descriptive Paragraphs:
ESTABLISHING ATMOSPHERE

> Goal: Use imagery and precise wording to establish atmosphere.

➡ Get Set

Atmosphere is the general feeling or mood created through a piece of writing. In a quick go-around, ask students to name various moods they've experienced over the past few days, and the events that brought about these moods. List their responses on the board. For example: *cheerful/My report card was the best ever.*

➡ Go

Point out that writers create atmosphere through imagery, metaphors, word choice, and so on. Enter one of the moods from the chart in the center of an idea web like the one shown in the reproducible on page 112. Challenge the class to brainstorm vivid words and phrases to complete the web and create the atmosphere.

Distribute the reproducible and have students work in small groups to complete the idea web. Then have them draft a paragraph based on the idea web.

➡ Follow Up

Suggest that students work independently to write a personal sketch based on a recollection from their own lives, a place whose atmosphere they remember vividly, or an event that evoked strong feelings.

Tip Leave it up to students whether to share this personal sketch with a writing partner, but make sure they file their work in their Writing Folders.

Descriptive Writing

Name _____ Date _____

Organizing Descriptive Paragraphs:
ESTABLISHING ATMOSPHERE

Event or setting we will describe:

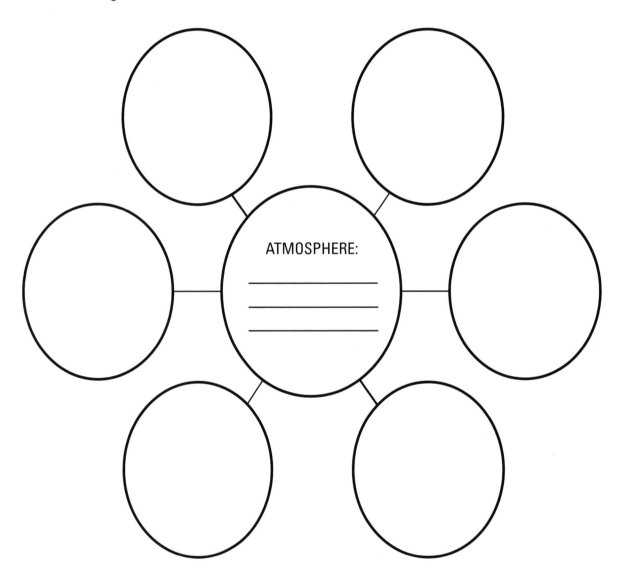

ATMOSPHERE:

_____

_____

_____

Organizing Descriptive Paragraphs :
WIND-UP

Tall tales, with their exaggerations and grandiose descriptions, are a natural form for students to use as they apply what they know about descriptive writing. Display the reproducible on page 114 and review the elements of a tall tale.

Post a set of guidelines that focus on the descriptive techniques students have studied. For example:

- Use position words to convey the placement of the characters in the setting.
- Show the sequence of events with time-order words.
- Describe characters and their exaggerated qualities, appearance, and skills. Use metaphors, similes, and personification.
- Reveal the characters through their actions and speech. Include dialogue.
- Establish the atmosphere of your tall tale.

Descriptive Writing

100 Writing Lessons © by Tara McCarthy • Scholastic Teaching Resources

Name_____ Date _____

Organizing Descriptive Paragraphs :
WIND-UP

A tall tale is a humorous story in which the qualities of a hero are exaggerated: *Slue-Foot Sue rode down the Rio Grande on a catfish that was as big as a whale.*

Write about the further adventures of your favorite tall-tale hero, or create an original character to write about. There's a catch—your tall tale has to be set in the 21st century. To plan your tall tale, complete the chart below.

A TALL TALE:_____

Setting: Time: Now Place:_____	Characters	Problem	Events	Solution

Descriptive Writing

Name_____ Date _____

On Your Own:
WORDS THAT LOOK LIKE THEMSELVES

What comes to your mind when you hear the words *cloud* and *rock*? White, puffy clouds on a sunny summer day? The dark, swirling clouds of a rainstorm? Hard blocks of stone cut from the ground? Round pebbles at the bottom of a stream?

Choose one of the words in the box below. What images pop into your head when you see or say the word? Write the word to make it look like what it represents.

rainbow	popcorn	umbrella	highway	mountain
marshmallow	football	lightning	cactus	teeth

Descriptive Writing

Descriptive Writing

Name_____ Date _____

On Your Own: UNUSUAL HOMES!

A. Remember the nursery rhyme about the old woman who lived in a shoe? Imagine a land where houses are shaped like flowers, oranges, lunchboxes, envelopes, socks, or other distinctly "unhouselike" objects.

What does one of those houses look like? Think about the following ideas:

- Who might live in the house?
- What does it look like from the outside and the inside?
- What does the house smell like inside?
- How do the walls, ceiling, and floors feel when you touch them?
- What sounds do you hear around the house?

B. Draw a picture of the house. Label the details in your picture to help describe it.

Descriptive Writing

Name _____ Date _____

On Your Own:
"WANTED" POSTERS AND FLYERS

Make a "Wanted" poster for a nonhuman entity. Your poster—like the real ones in post offices—should give explicit data about what observant citizens should be on the look-out for, and should feature an illustration. See the example to the right.

WANTED: RAINBOW

Wears many colors. Is likely to hang out in the sky but also has been seen in puddles and prisms. Especially likes moist weather. Favorite costume is a huge arc, reaching like a bending bridge from horizon to horizon. Disappears suddenly, fading like a dream! If sighted, notify artists and crayon manufacturers.

If you're having trouble thinking of an idea, consider the following possible subjects for "Wanted" posters:

- spring (or any of the seasons)
- the moon
- a hug
- an icicle

- the smell of pine trees
- the taste of your favorite ice cream
- a favorite toy that you lost a long time ago

Descriptive Writing

Name _____ Date _____

On Your Own: HAIKUS ABOUT TIME

A haiku is a form of Japanese poetry that has the following structure:

- **First line:** five syllables
- **Second line:** seven syllables
- **Third line:** five syllables

Write a haiku that describes an event in sequence. Here are some examples:

> First, gold sun rising.
> At noon, clouds hover on hills.
> At night, the storm breaks.

> Geese fly in moonlight.
> Soon, frogs croak in moonlit ponds.
> Now the spring moon smiles!

Before you read aloud your haiku to the class, ask your audience to imagine that the events are unfolding in time order.

Descriptive Writing

Name_____ Date _____

On Your Own:

DESCRIBING STAGE SETTINGS

The setting of a play is usually described from the viewpoint of the actors as they enter and move about the stage, not from the viewpoint of the audience. For example, "stage left" means the actor's left; "stage right" means the actor's right.

Study the description of the setting for a stage presentation of Cinderella.

Title of Play: Cinderella

Act 1

Setting: A large kitchen in an old house. At stage left is a door opening to the rest of the house. At stage right is a door opening to the outside. At the center of the stage is a stone fireplace, where a fire burns brightly. A coal scuttle, two well-used brooms, and a mop are leaning against the hearth. A kettle hangs over the fire. To the left of the hearth is a rickety rocking chair in which Cinderella is sitting as the curtain opens. The whole stage is light dimly—the fire casts a strong, golden glow.

Write the setting for Act 1 of a play. For the play, use a piece of your own writing, a favorite story by another author, or create a new story.

Descriptive Writing

Name _____ Date _____

On Your Own: RATE YOURSELF

1. For you, what's the most challenging or hardest thing about descriptive writing?

_____

_____

_____

_____

2. For you, what's the easiest thing about descriptive writing?

_____

_____

_____

_____

3. Of all the descriptive writing you've done in this section, which piece pleases you the most? Why?

_____

_____

_____

_____

4. Of all the descriptive writing you've done in this section, which pleases you the least? Why?

_____

_____

_____

_____

Descriptive Writing

Composition: SENTENCES

Present sentence structure and sentence combining in its real-life, writerly context: to make descriptions more compelling and effective. There are two basic strategies for students to experiment with this context. One is to combine sentences to stress major images. The other is to write sentences that reflect the pace of the actions the writer is describing. Before beginning the lesson, hand out the reproducible on page 122.

Combining Sentences

Write the following pair of sentences on the board and ask students to identify the vivid descriptive words and phrases in each sentence. Underline their responses.

> A *frightened* dog *snarled* and *bolted into the underbrush*.
> The dog was *skinny* and *coated with mud.*

Then challenge the class to combine the images into a single sentence and write them on the board. There will be various ways to do this. Here are some examples:

> *The skinny dog, snarling, frightened, and coated with mud, bolted into the underbrush.*
> *The frightened, skinny, snarling, mud-coated dog bolted into the underbrush.*

Give students time to study the examples of combined sentences on the reproducible.

Sentences That Reflect the Pace

Write the following topics on the board. Discuss which topics suggest abrupt, short movements and which suggest ongoing, flowing movement:

- autumn leaves drifting down trees (ongoing, flowing)
- a windstorm in a forest (abrupt, short)
- playing hopscotch (abrupt, short)
- listening to calm music (ongoing, flowing)

After students have correctly categorized the examples, have them look at the example of the car with engine problems on the reproducible. Ask: *How do the lengths of the sentences contribute to the image of the event?*

More Practice

In a brainstorm session, have students list some recent events or situations they've experienced at home or at school, such as a power outage, a stray cat or dog at the door, lost homework, babysitting experiences. Ask students to write independently on a topic, keeping in mind sentence combining and relating sentences to the pace of the action.

Descriptive Writing

Name _____ Date _____

Composition: SENTENCES

You can combine sentences to emphasize major events—and combining descriptive words and phrases can make your sentences grown-up and writerly.

Separate sentences:

Wild water gushed under the fragile bridge.
The bridge swayed.

Possibilities for combining sentences:

Wild water gushed under the fragile, swaying bridge.
The fragile bridge swayed as the wild water gushed under it.

You can adjust sentence length to capture the movement and action you're describing. Notice how these sentences reflect the pace of the actions the writer is describing.

Sentences showing abrupt, short movement:

The car choked. Gushes of steam poured out. Rattles rumbled from the engine. A gassy odor wafted over me.

Sentences showing ongoing, flowing movement:

The soft water held me as I floated sleepily on its surface, lapped in the lullaby whisper of the gentle waves.

---

100 Writing Lessons © by Tara McCarthy • Scholastic Teaching Resources

Composition: PUNCTUATING DIALOGUE

Like Alice in *Alice in Wonderland*, most young people like stories "with conversations in them." Consequently, they like to put conversations into their own stories. As long as the dialogue serves a purpose—the words reveal something about a character or move along the plot—it can be a strong descriptive technique. However, in addition to using language precisely, a writer has to use punctuation precisely so it's always clear to the reader who is speaking.

Distribute the reproducible on page 124 to students and display it on the overhead. Go over the rules and ask students to give another example for each one. Either write the example on the board, guided in the punctuation by students, or have students write the examples.

More Practice

Divide the class into groups of four or five. Further divide the groups into pairs or trios. Let each smaller group take turns acting out a scene. The audience will work together to record the dialogue and action. Suggest that each group jot down the speech and movement and then use their notes to compose and punctuate complete sentences that might appear in a story.

Descriptive Writing

Name_____ Date _____

Composition: PUNCTUATING DIALOGUE

When you use dialogue, be sure to follow these punctuation rules.

DON'T WORRY NOTE: Don't worry about these rules too much as you draft your writing. Do use the rules as you edit and proofread with a writing partner.

RULE	EXAMPLE
1. Put quotation marks around the words the character says. Always capitalize the first word.	Aunt Em said, "Here's my photo album."
2. Use a comma to set off the dialogue from the rest of the sentence.	I said, "I'd like to look at it."
3. Put a period, question mark, or exclamation mark inside the quotation mark.	She said, "Do you recognize any of these people?" "No!" I said.
4. Dialogue is sometimes divided. • If the dialogue consists of one sentence, put the first comma inside the first part and the second comma outside the second part. • If the dialogue consists of two sentences, begin the second sentence with a capital letter.	"This is your grandpa," said Aunt Em, "and this is me!" "Photo albums are fun," I said. "These pictures tell me about my family."
5. If more than one character is speaking, begin each character's words with a new paragraph.	_____ "Aren't you studying family histories in school?" _____ "We sure are!" I said.
6. Don't confuse direct quotations (speech) with indirect quotations (thoughts). Don't use quotation marks in indirect quotations.	"I'll let you take this album to school," said Aunt Em. "First promise me you'll keep it safe!" My aunt said I could take the album to school if I promised to keep it safe.

100 Writing Lessons © by Tara McCarthy • Scholastic Teaching Resources

Writing Across the Curriculum:
WRITING ABOUT
SCIENCE AND TECHNOLOGY

While "science writing" is basically expository, writers can use descriptive writing techniques to make this type of writing vivid and precise. By teaching these techniques, you can help students come to accept and enjoy writing as a natural follow-up to the observations, procedures, and conclusions related to their science activities.

Model how you might make a science report more descriptive:

The Draft:
Rocks
We collected rocks and stones. The rocks had different shapes and textures.

The Revision:
Rock Histories and Mysteries
<u>Our geology group</u> collected <u>ten different</u> rocks and stones. Some of the rocks were smooth and almost silky, while others were <u>jagged and rough</u>.

With students, brainstorm a list of familiar science and technology subjects they could describe, such as the metamorphosis of a butterfly, how a hybrid car works, what happens during a solar/lunar eclipse, and so on. Then work with the class in composing a paragraph about the subject that is rich in description.

Write About Science

Distribute the reproducible on page 126. Ask students to use it to write about a phenomenon they can readily describe through observation or investigation.

Establish some simple criteria such as the following and ask pairs to use the criteria as they share and discuss their work:
- The steps must follow a sequence.
- All the main steps are recorded.
- Descriptive words and phrases make the steps clear and interesting to the reader.

Descriptive Writing

Name_____ Date _____

100 Writing Lessons © by Tara McCarthy • Scholastic Teaching Resources

Across the Curriculum: WRITING ABOUT SCIENCE AND TECHNOLOGY

A. Choose one of the scientific topics below to write about—or think of one of your own.

- weather
- how pets indicate their needs
- how a remote-control works
- star-sightings and formations
- how a compass works
- traffic patterns

B. Write down the guidelines the teacher gives you.

Guidelines: _____

_____

_____

_____

_____

C. Make your writing as descriptive as you can so your readers can visualize and understand the subject.

SCIENTIFIC TOPIC:

Expository Writing

Expository Writing

Main Idea: START WITH "HOW MANY"

> ### Goal: Overcome the "I-don't-have-anything-to-write-about" syndrome.

➡ Get Set

For many students, the task of writing is easier when they know up-front "how many" they have to write about, as in "Four Great Books I've Read This Year" or "Three Main Attractions at the Mall."

Write such a heading on the board and call on students to list the appropriate number of examples. Then act as a scribe as students rephrase the heading as a topic sentence and the examples as supporting sentences.

> There are three main attractions at our local mall. The first one is the three-speed merry-go-round that's just been installed. The second is the new computer store. The third is the book store where authors come and read their books aloud.

➡ Go

Distribute the reproducible on page129. Encourage students to work independently on all three parts.

➡ Follow Up

Pair students who have written on the same subject. As partners share and compare their work, they'll usually discover that they've come up with a variety of ideas. Editing and rewriting are optional.

> **Tip** Some students who claim to have nothing to write about can write quite a bit if they begin with the following topic sentence: *I have nothing to write about because...*

Expository Writing

Name _____ Date _____

Main Idea: START WITH "HOW MANY"

A. Choose and circle one of the following topics:

Four Strange Animals   Three Ridiculous TV Shows

Five Great Holidays   Six Frightening Things

Four Online Time-Wasters   Five Sports Superstars

B. Write a topic sentence for your topic.

_____

_____

C. Write and number examples that support your topic sentence.

_____

_____

_____

_____

_____

D. On the lines below and/or on the back of this sheet, write a paragraph on your topic. Begin with your topic sentence. Then follow with sentences that present the supporting examples.

_____

_____

_____

_____

_____

_____

_____

_____

100 Writing Lessons © by Tara McCarthy • Scholastic Teaching Resources

Expository Writing

Main Idea: NO IDEA IS TOO SMALL

> Goal: Discover significant ideas in "small" ones.

➡ Get Set

Distribute the reproducible on page 131. Ask students to write the word *car* on the Idea line. Then have each student list up to ten words or brief phrases that come to mind about a car. Allow four to five minutes for this step; give a "one-minute left" warning.

> A. Idea: Car
> 1. riding in the backseat
> 2. car radio
> 3. flat tire

➡ Go

Each student chooses what he or she considers the least important idea or image on the list and writes it as the title on the reproducible. Then students write for five to ten minutes (gauge writing time to your class's abilities), beginning with the following opener: *I am in a car and ...*

Their writing can flow over to the back of the reproducible sheet.

> I am in a car and the radio is tuned to the all-news station. The announcer says there's a big traffic tie-up on the bridge. I get nervous! Will we get to the fair in time for the parade?

➡ Follow Up

- Talk about how an idea that seems of little importance at first can lead to an interesting piece of writing. That is, no idea is too small or unimportant.

- Writing comes alive for the writer when it's read aloud. So invite students to read their paragraphs from the reproducible to one another. The audience should not comment, but just listen attentively.

Tip You can repeat this activity using *-ing* forms of active verbs, e.g., ***running, crying, laughing, eating, watching***.

Expository Writing

Name _____ Date _____

Main Idea: NO IDEA IS TOO SMALL

A. Idea: _____

1. _____   6. _____
2. _____   7. _____
3. _____   8. _____
4. _____   9. _____
5. _____   10. _____

B. Title: _____

_____

_____

_____

_____

_____

_____

_____

_____

_____

_____

_____

_____

_____

_____

100 Writing Lessons © by Tara McCarthy • Scholastic Teaching Resources

Expository Writing

Main Idea: FOCUS ON YESTERDAY

Goal: Build on recent experiences.

➡ Get Set

Distribute the reproducible on page 133 and read the A heading: 10 events I remember from yesterday. As the previous activity (pages 130–131) emphasized, no idea is too small. Allow four to five minutes for students to list their recollections.

> 10 events I remember from yesterday
>
> 1. The school bus was late.
> 2. I forgot my lunch.
> 3. The teacher complimented me on my science report.

➡ Go

Have students choose what they consider the least important event and write it on the title line in section B of the reproducible. For about five minutes, students free-write about this event, beginning with the topic sentence: I remember . . .

> The school bus was late.
>
> I remember that the school bus was late, and I felt very angry because we were all standing in the rain just waiting and waiting.

➡ Follow Up

Encourage partners to read one another's paragraphs aloud. This gives writers a chance to critique their own work silently.

Tip To get kids thinking about the power of writing, ask the following question: *Where is the idea for your story now—only in your head, on a sheet of paper, or also in the heads of people who've heard it?*

100 Writing Lessons

Expository Writing

Name _____ Date _____

Main Idea: FOCUS ON YESTERDAY

A. 10 events I remember from yesterday...

1. _____ 2. _____

3. _____ 4. _____

5. _____ 6. _____

7. _____ 8. _____

9. _____ 10. _____

B. Title: _____

I remember _____

_____

_____

_____

_____

_____

_____

_____

_____

_____

_____

_____

_____

100 Writing Lessons © by Tara McCarthy • Scholastic Teaching Resources

Expository Writing

Main Idea: SUMMARIZE MAIN POINTS

Goal: Zero in on the 5 Ws.

➡ Get Set

Ask five or six students to sit in a circle. In 45 seconds or less, each student summarizes a story or article he or she has read by identifying the 5 Ws—Who, What, When, Where, Why. Set a timer so you can stop each student at exactly 45 seconds. Then call on the next student to give a summary. Model an example such as the following:

> [Who, Where] *In the story "The Ugly Duckling," a peculiar-looking bird hatches in a nest of ducklings in a farmyard.* [Why] *The ducklings make fun of him because his appearance and behavior differ greatly from their own.* [What] *But as he grows, the strange duckling begins to show a wonderful grace and elegance. In fact, he is a swan that has hatched in the duck nest by mistake.* [When] *Soon the young swan flies away, looking far handsomer than a duck could ever hope to be.*

➡ Go

Briefly discuss the activity by posing questions such as *What was fun about this activity? What was difficult? If you could do your summary over again, how would you change it?* Distribute the reproducible on page 135 and have students complete it independently.

➡ Follow Up

Ask students to write a paragraph using the data they've supplied in their reproducibles. Invite them to read aloud their work.

> **Tip** The physical act of writing—just moving a pen or pencil over a page—is sometimes as important a warm-up as creating original content. So, if a student is reluctant to write a summary of a new story, suggest simply rewording the summary you presented as an example.

Expository Writing

Name _____ Date _____

Main Idea: SUMMARIZE MAIN POINTS

Summarize the main points of a favorite story or article in the boxes below.

WHO?
WHAT?
WHERE?
WHEN?
WHY?

100 Writing Lessons © by Tara McCarthy • Scholastic Teaching Resources

Expository Writing

Main Idea: DEVELOP THE MAIN IDEA

Goal: Organize supporting details.

➡ Get Set

Display the reproducible on page 137 and model how to fill it out: *In the center circle, I'll write a broad subject: Important Activities Outside School. Can you help me name four activities? I'll write them in the squares: sports, having fun with friends, doing homework, helping out at home. Now, in the small circles connected to each square, I want to list specific examples. Can you name two specific examples of what you do when you have fun with friends? That's great—playing a computer game and skateboarding.*

Point out to students that they've gone from a broad subject, or main idea, to increasingly more specific examples, or supporting details.

➡ Go

Pass out copies of the reproducible for partners to complete or to copy on a separate sheet of paper. Possible main ideas include Environmental Concerns, Problems in Our School, Ways to Use My Allowance, Good Choices in Forming Friendships.

➡ Follow Up

Ask partners to show their completed graphic organizers on an overhead projector and discuss them with the rest of the class. Focus comments on the positive aspects of each pair's work, pointing out how they narrowed down the topic.

Tip Encourage students to put their completed graphic organizers in a folder titled "Writing Perks." Remind them to use the material in the folder when they're thinking about topics for expository writing.

Expository Writing

Name _____ Date _____

Main Idea: DEVELOP THE MAIN IDEA

Use the graphic organizer to develop a main idea.

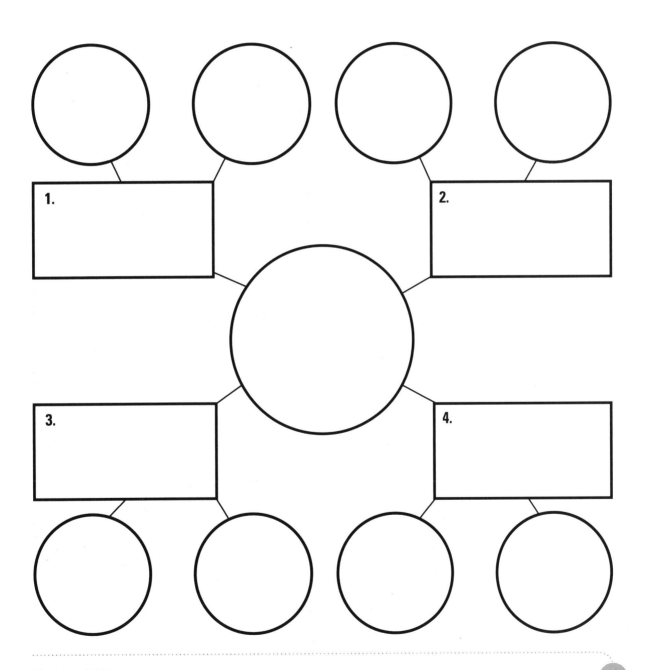

Expository Writing

Expository Writing

Main Idea: WRITE A TOPIC SENTENCE

Goal: State a main idea concisely.

➡ Get Set

On the board or an overhead, display a paragraph that lacks a topic sentence.

> Some students demonstrated science projects they'd worked on all year long. Other students gave readers theater productions of favorite books. One group of students read their own short stories aloud. Some kids who'd done a community history project showed their videos of local historical sites.

Help students identify the main idea (e.g., Students presented their best work.). Then work with them to state it as an introductory or topic sentence (e.g., *To share their best work with other classrooms, students showed examples of what they had accomplished.*) Write the newly created topic sentence in front of the paragraph above.

➡ Go

Hand out copies of the reproducible on page 139. Read aloud the paragraph in section A. Discuss possible topic sentences, and then have students choose one to write on the reproducible. For example: *Our school has facilities for kids who are interested in different sports.* Then have students complete section B of the reproducible independently.

Tip Write word groups such as the ones shown below on the board. Ask kids to suggest what category, or main idea, each group might represent. Encourage them to play with the main idea and create a topic sentence for a paragraph-to-be.

- thunder, lightning, blizzards, tornadoes
- skateboard, rollerblade, baby carriage, scooter

Expository Writing

Name _____ Date _____

Main Idea: WRITE A TOPIC SENTENCE

A. Write a topic sentence for the paragraph below.

_____

_____

_____

For example, we have an outdoor track for sprinters and a playing field adaptable to soccer, baseball, or football. For kids turned on to archery, we have a field set aside for that. There's also a putting green for golfers.

B. Choose three subjects from the box below and circle them. Write a topic sentence that could be a snappy, attention-grabbing lead for a paragraph about each subject.

Why Lots of TV Shows Fail	Impossible Assignments
School Lunch Problems	The Ideal Teacher
School Fads	Peculiar Pets

My Topic Sentences:

1. _____

_____

2. _____

_____

3. _____

_____

Main Idea : WIND-UP

To review how writers support main ideas with supporting details, show a pyramid graphic organizer on the board or an overhead.

Main Idea:

After-school

activities for kids

Supporting Idea:

Community outreach activities

to help senior citizens

Supporting Idea:

Sports practice

Supporting Idea:

Using catch-up room to do homework

Supporting Idea:

Practicing computer skills at the Youth Center

Distribute the reproducible on page 141. Ask students to choose a subject and then fill in the pyramid. Suggest that they draft a paragraph based on their completed pyramid.

Expository Writing

Name _____ Date _____

Main Idea : WIND-UP

Choose a main idea from the list below, or think of one of your own. Complete the pyramid with four supporting ideas.

- Great Birthday Plans
- School Rules We Need
- School Bus Drivers' Problems
- Helping New Students

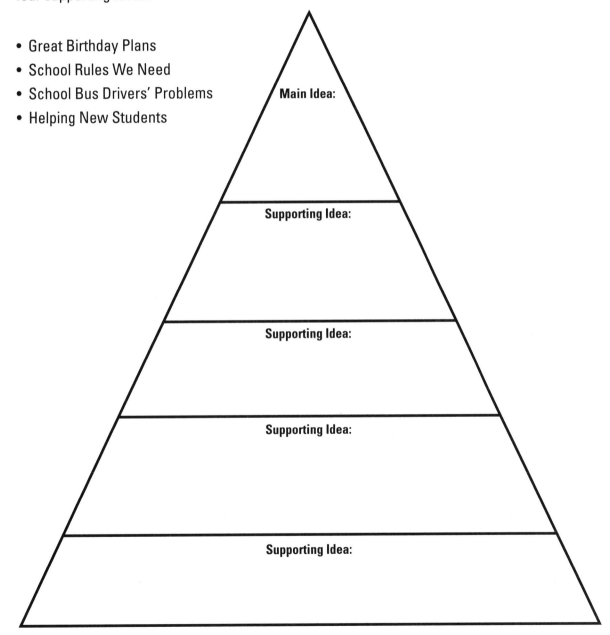

Main Idea:

Supporting Idea:

Supporting Idea:

Supporting Idea:

Supporting Idea:

Expository Writing

Purpose: SHOW HOW THINGS HAPPEN

> Goal: Link causes and effects.

Get Set

Ask students to listen for cause and effect as you read the following old poem aloud:

Because of a nail the shoe was lost.
Because of a shoe the horse was lost.
Because of the horse the rider was lost.
Because of the rider the message was lost.
Because of the message the battle was lost.
Because of the battle the kingdom was lost.
And all for the loss of a horseshoe nail!

Then display the cause-effect wheel on the reproducible on page 143. Work with the class to complete it.

Go

Distribute the reproducible on page 144. After previewing the words in the box and the directions, ask partners to carry out the activity.

Follow Up

Invite students to use their cause-effect wheels as the basis for a poem.

Tip In a fast go-round, present sentence starters like the following, which include useful cause-and-effect words and phrases from the box on page 144:

- I didn't do my homework because …
- The game was called off due to …
- The dog ate the birthday cake, and as a result, …
- The UFO landed in my yard; consequently, …

Call on students to complete the sentences quickly. Wild and funny endings are welcome.

Expository Writing

Name _____ Date _____

Purpose: SHOW HOW THINGS HAPPEN

Complete the cause-effect wheel.

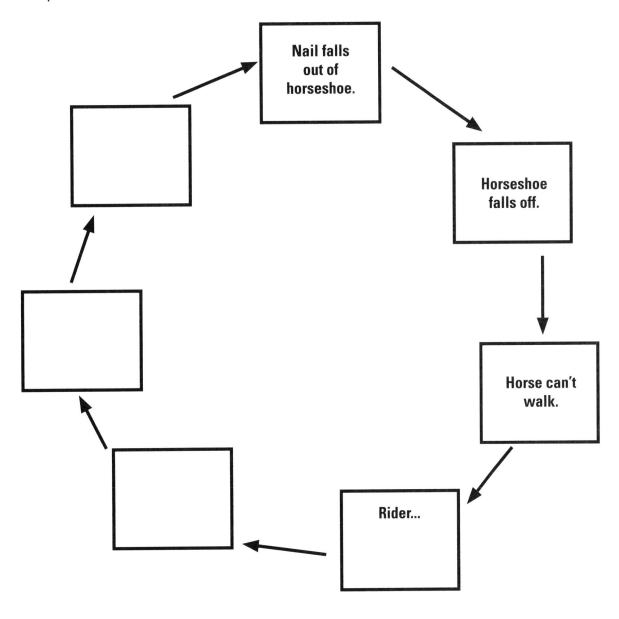

Nail falls out of horseshoe.

Horseshoe falls off.

Horse can't walk.

Rider...

Expository Writing

Name _____ Date _____

Purpose: SHOW HOW THINGS HAPPEN

A. With your partner, choose one of the beginning situations below and discuss what might follow. Use some words from the box in your discussion.

Beginning situations:

- A mouse got into the house.
- I forgot to close the window.
- Your teacher won a million dollars in the lottery.
- A tornado headed for your town.
- The school bus got a flat tire and also ran out of gas.

B. In the space below or on the back of this sheet, make a cause-effect wheel that resulted from your discussion.

> **Some Useful Cause-and-Effect Words**
> so
> because
> led to
> for this reason
> then
> consequently
> if
> when
> as a result
> caused by
> due to

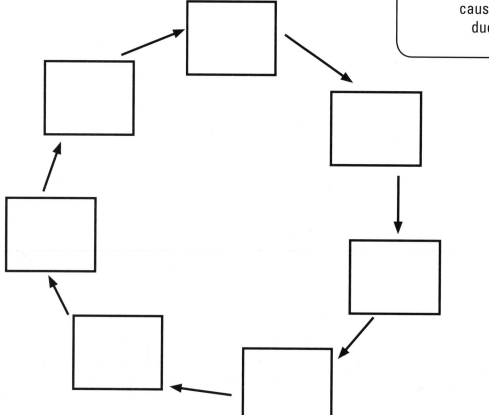

100 Writing Lessons © by Tara McCarthy • Scholastic Teaching Resources

Expository Writing

Purpose: NOTE THE SIMILARITIES AND DIFFERENCES

Goal: Compare and contrast members of a category.

➡ Get Set

Ahead of time, write common plural nouns like those below on separate index cards, one card per student.

birds	socks	lunches	cars	houses	gifts	parties
leaves	shells	trees	friends	cats	kitchens	

Distribute the reproducible on page 146 and read aloud the comparison and contrast words. Write the word *shoes* on the board. With the class, develop a paragraph comparing and contrasting shoes and using some of the comparison and contrast words. Here's an example.

> Shoes are outer coverings for people's feet. In general, shoes have durable soles on the bottom for protection, and tops that secure the shoe to the foot. However, other than that, shoes are different in several ways. For example, shoes may be made of leather, natural fibers, rubber, or materials made by humans. There are shoes for different activities, such as...

➡ Go

Place the index cards face down on a desk or table and have each student select one. Tell students to use the lines in Section B of the reproducible to write for five minutes to compare and contrast items in the category on their card. Remind them to use some of the comparison and contrast words on the reproducible.

➡ Follow Up

Form groups of five or six students and have the members of each group read aloud their work. Urge the audience to listen carefully so they'll be able to make comments and to think about questions such as *What are the main similarities and differences that the writer states? What comparison and contrast words does the writer use?*

Tip Some students may have more success in writing about similarities and differences between pairs such as the following: door/window, sun/moon, pen/pencil, cat/dog, TV/radio, car/truck, shoes/gloves and lake/ocean.

Expository Writing

Name _____ Date _____

Purpose: NOTE THE SIMILARITIES
                    AND DIFFERENCES

A. You can use the words in the box to help you compare and contrast.

Some Comparison and Contrast Words			
alike	but	in general	have in common
similar	both	in contrast	on the other hand
same	also	different	in the same way
unlike	however	differences	instead

B. Write a paragraph comparing and contrasting the items in the category listed on the card you drew. Remember to use comparison and contrast words.

_____

_____

_____

_____

_____

_____

_____

_____

_____

_____

_____

Expository Writing

Purpose: DEFINE AND DEVELOP

> Goal: Write a paragraph to define and develop a situation.

⮕ Get Set

Give each student a copy of the reproducible on page 148. Call their attention to the title and definition in Section A. Invite students to read aloud the chart examples and discuss the specific threats to each animal.

⮕ Go

Remember that copying is a good way for students to begin writing. Write the following topic sentence on the board and ask students to copy it on the first line under the B section of the reproducible: *An endangered animal is one that is in danger of extinction, often due to human activity.* Then direct students to choose three examples of human activity from the chart in Section A and use them to create sentences that support the topic sentence.

⮕ Follow Up

Have students work in small groups to read aloud their paragraphs. Suggest they ask questions such as the following: *Does each sentence strongly support the topic sentence? What is my best sentence? Why is it effective? Which sentence could I rewrite to make it stronger?*

Tip Suggest the following subjects for additional practice:
- In your own words, define the word *friendship*. Develop and support your definition.
- What are some differences between (choose one)
  - relaxing and loafing?
  - a joke and a trick?
  - a contest and a fight?
- What are the qualities of a great book? List the qualities and give some examples from great books you've read.

Expository Writing

Name _____ Date _____

Purpose: DEFINE AND DEVELOP

A. Title: Six of the Most Endangered Animals

Definition: *Endangered* describes animals that are in danger of extinction.

Animal	Approximate Number Left	Threat to Survival
1. Monk seal	400	Pollution from oil, sewage, industrial chemicals
2. Mountain gorilla	400	Destruction of forest habitat; hunting for body parts
3. Siberian tiger	250–400	Hunting for body parts
4. Javan rhinoceros	70	Hunting for tusks; destruction of habitat
5. Giant panda	1,000	Destruction of habitat
6. Yangtze River dolphin	150	River pollution

B. Write a paragraph about human activities that put animals in danger of extinction.

Topic sentence:

_____

_____

For example, _____

_____

_____

_____

_____

_____

_____

_____

_____

_____

_____

Expository Writing

Purpose: GO FROM START TO FINISH

Goal: List steps in sequence.

➡ Get Set

Organize students into groups of five or six and assign one of the following topics to each group:

How to Miss the School Bus	How to Avoid Homework
How to Be Popular	How to Impress Your Teacher
How to Make a Super Sandwich	How to Ride a Bike

Distribute the reproducible on page 150 to each student and go over the directions with the class.

➡ Go

Have group members work together to 1) write the steps for the "How to..." on the reproducible, and 2) develop those steps into a "how-to" paragraph.

➡ Follow Up

Tell each group to appoint a member to read aloud his or her paragraphs from Section B of the reproducible to the class. Audience feedback should address sequence, completeness, and clarity. Have groups revise their paragraphs according to the audience comments.

Tip Students who need practice in understanding English sequence words benefit from physically carrying out an ordinary classroom chore, such as "how to clean out a desk," with you. Limit the sequence to four or five operations. Use sequence words—*first, then, next, second, third, finally,* and so on—as you and the students carry out the chore. Wind up by having these students orally recap the steps of the chore in order (e.g., *First, take out all the papers from the middle drawer. Then, divide the papers into old stuff and new stuff. Next,...*).

Expository Writing

Name _____ Date _____

Purpose: GO FROM START TO FINISH

Our topic: How to _____

A. Your how-to should have at least five steps. Write the steps in sequence in the footprints. You can draw more footprints to add more steps if necessary.

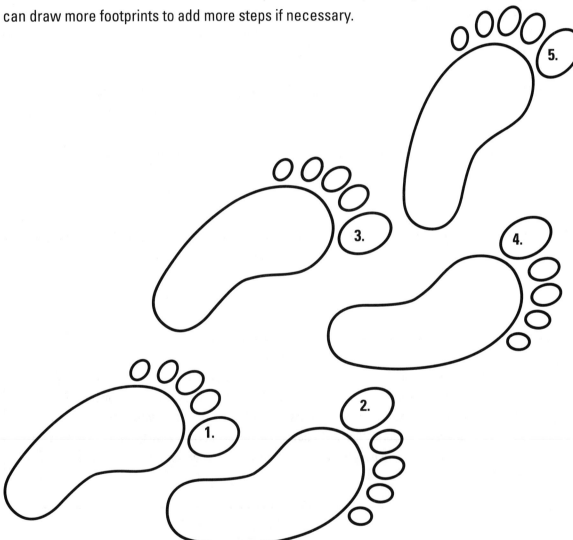

B. On the back of this sheet or on a separate sheet of paper, write a how-to paragraph based on the steps in Section A.

100 Writing Lessons © by Tara McCarthy • Scholastic Teaching Resources

Expository Writing

Purpose: EXPLAIN THE GAME

Goal: Provide the essentials of an activity.

➡ Get Set

Hand out the reproducible on page 152 and explain that the Fact Profile gives the essentials of a professional game. Work with students to find the appropriate heading for each entry. (Answers: 1. How Do You Play It? 2. What's the Aim? 3. How Many Players? 4. Players' Positions 5. Game Time 6. Key Rules) Then ask students to identify the game (professional basketball) and write it at the top of the reproducible. Discuss how the details in the Fact Profile led to the identification.

➡ Go

Distribute the reproducible on page 153 to pairs of students. Tell partners to think of a well-known game and fill in data about it on the reproducible. Remind students that their explanation should not identify the game by name but should provide clear and precise details about it.

➡ Follow Up

Have partners read aloud the steps in their game. Stress that winners in this activity are writers who make the steps so clear that the identification of the game is easy; i.e., an accurate first guess means the explanation was great!

Tip Create a list of these sequence words and phrases for your students.

first	later	eventually	while
next	soon	finally	in the meantime
then	after	now	during

Expository Writing

Name _____ Date _____

Purpose: EXPLAIN THE GAME

Fact Profile for the Game of _____

1. _____

Bounce a large ball and throw it to each other as you move around.

2. _____

Score points by putting the ball into the opposing team's basket.

3. _____

There are five players on each team. Substitutes are allowed.

4. _____

Forwards play near the sides, centers stay near the basket, and guards play in the middle.

5. _____

The game lasts for four quarters. Each quarter is 12 minutes long. Teams can ask for one-minute time-outs.

6. _____

A player can move freely while bouncing the ball, but can take only one step while holding it. It's a personal foul to push an opponent. An opponent can only stand in the free-throw area for three seconds.

Write the headings where they belong in the Fact Profile.

Game Time	What's the Aim?	Players' Positions
How Do You Play It?	Key Rules	How Many Players?

Expository Writing

Name _____ Date _____

Purpose: EXPLAIN THE GAME

Give the details of a game without naming it. Use the headings below or write some of your own. Either way, keep the steps in order.

1. How Do You Play It?_____

_____

_____

2. What's the Aim? _____

_____

_____

3. How Many Players?_____

_____

_____

4. Players' Positions _____

_____

_____

5. Game Time _____

_____

_____

6. Key Rules _____

_____

_____

Finally, for the people guessing in your audience...

the game is _____

100 Writing Lessons © by Tara McCarthy • Scholastic Teaching Resources

Expository Writing

Purpose: WIND-UP

On the board or overhead, display the graphic organizer below. Talk about the problem and the purpose. Help students come up with possible solutions, with a plus and minus point for each. See the example below.

> *Solution 1: Enlarge the school. Plus: more classrooms; minus: raise local taxes to pay for the expansion.*
>
> *Solution 2: Stagger school hours. Plus: fewer students per class; minus: longer hours for school personnel.*
>
> *Solution 3: Bus some students to schools with empty classroom space. Plus: low cost; minus: students travel long distances to unfamiliar neighborhoods.*

Next, ask the class to decide on a solution and justify its choice.

PROBLEM: The classrooms at School X are too crowded.

OUR PURPOSE: Suggest possible solutions to the problem.

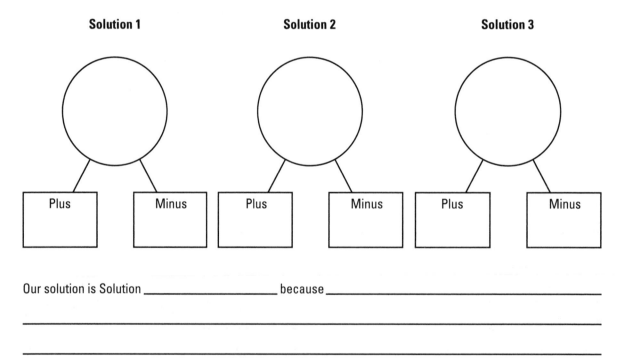

Our solution is Solution _____ because _____

_____

_____

Distribute the reproducible on page 155. Direct partners to choose a problem from the box. Have each partner complete the graphic organizer independently. Then pairs come together again to share, compare, and revise their graphic organizers. If partners wish, they can share their graphic organizers with their classmates.

Expository Writing

Name _____ Date _____

Purpose: WIND-UP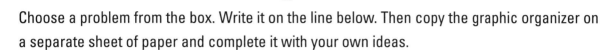

Choose a problem from the box. Write it on the line below. Then copy the graphic organizer on a separate sheet of paper and complete it with your own ideas.

> **PROBLEMS**
> - There is a severe water shortage in the community.
> - Skateboarders and pedestrians get in each other's way in the park.
> - There's no quiet place to do homework after school.
> - The town has no low-cost housing for senior citizens.
> - School cafeteria lunchtimes are too hurried and crowded.

PROBLEM: _____

OUR PURPOSE: Suggest possible solutions to the problem.

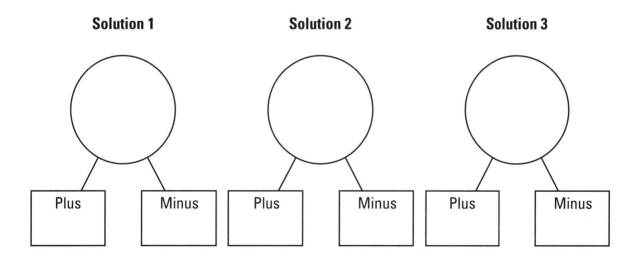

Our choice is Solution _____ because _____

_____

_____

Expository Writing

Audience: TALK TO YOURSELF

Goal: Practice reflection (writing just for yourself).

➡ Get Set

Talk with students about some of the day-to-day writing we do with only ourselves as the intended audience, e.g., homework notes, shopping lists, reminders (Don't forget to feed the cat!). Pose the following questions: *When you're writing just for yourself, is your writing the same or different as when you're writing for others? What are some of the differences?* Students may mention differences in neatness, punctuation, style, and even the kind of paper they use.

➡ Go

Pass out the reproducible on page 157. Explain that another purpose of writing for yourself can be to capture ideas that you might use later. Ask students to select a topic from the box on the reproducible and free-write about it for five minutes. Stress the following:

- All your ideas count.
- Don't stop to make corrections.
- The writer is the sole audience. No one but you will see the results—unless you decide otherwise.

➡ Follow Up

After students complete the free-write, discuss the activity. Did they feel they knew more or less about their topic than they realized? Could they have written more on the topic if they had had more time? Ask students to read their writing to themselves and underline the most important ideas.

Tip You can turn this into a small-group activity. Tell the group to choose a topic from the box on the reproducible on page 157. Have students brainstorm on the topic, with you acting as the scribe/note-taker and prompting them as necessary. Read the results of the brainstorming aloud to the group. Comment on the diversity of ideas that students can recall from memory and create from their imagination.

Expository Writing

Name _____ Date _____

Audience: TALK TO YOURSELF

Choose a topic from the box. Free-write about it for five minutes.

the ocean	climates	endangered animals	space travel
noise pollution	collectibles	school fads	school rules
chores at home	new students	selecting a pet	advertisements

_____

_____

_____

_____

_____

_____

_____

_____

_____

_____

_____

100 Writing Lessons © by Tara McCarthy • Scholastic Teaching Resources

Expository Writing

Audience:
HAVE A WRITTEN CONVERSATION

Goal: Write informal messages.

➡ Get Set

Initiate a discussion about the forms of written messages we direct to people we know well, e.g., e-mail, friendly letters and cards, notes passed in class or written to family members. Ask: *How is writing for someone you know well different from writing just for yourself? How seriously do you pay attention to the rules of spelling and grammar for this type of writing? How clearly and neatly do you write?*

➡ Go

Ask students to work together, and distribute a copy of the reproducible on page 159 to each pair. After selecting a topic from the box on the reproducible, partners exchange messages on the subject. Each student will write a total of two messages.

➡ Follow Up

Invite partners to read aloud their messages to a small group. The audience should listen for and comment on the following:

- Is the topic clearly stated?
- Do all the sentences relate to the topic?
- What are the best parts of the message exchange? Which parts could use some improvement?

Tip Use the reproducible on page 159 to work with groups of three students. Write the first message and read it aloud to the group and then record each of the student's responses in sections 2–4. Discuss the clarity and style of the messages.

Expository Writing

Name _____ Date _____

 Audience:
HAVE A WRITTEN CONVERSATION

Choose a topic from the box below for your messages. Underline the topic.

homework	**a problem at school**	**a neighborhood mystery**
party plans	**vacation plans**	**an awful TV program**
a disappointment	**a success**	**a humorous event**

Write your messages below.

1: Original Message

From: _____

To: _____

_____

_____

2. Response to Message 1

From: _____

To: _____

_____

_____

3: Response to Message 2

From: _____

To: _____

_____

_____

4. Response to Message 3

From: _____

To: _____

_____

_____

Expository Writing

Audience: CORRESPOND WITH SOMEONE YOU KNOW

> Goal: Write about a topic to someone at a distance.

➡ Get Set

With your students, list some typical recipients of letters from home. These might include faraway relatives, friends who have moved away, or family members who travel a lot and like to be updated about what's going on at home. You might also discuss the fun of getting a letter or an e-mail from someone we don't see very often. What do students want to hear about when they receive letters—little stuff or big stuff? New stuff or old stuff?

➡ Go

Distribute the reproducible on page 161. Students may select a topic from Box 1 or come up with a topic of their own and then select a recipient from Box 2 or think of another recipient. Have students write a letter about their topic to the recipient.

➡ Follow Up

Ask students to share their letters in small groups. The audience should listen for the following:

- What is the topic?
- What are some great details that develop the topic?
- Do any details wander from the topic?
- What else might the recipient want to know about the topic?

Encourage students to revise their letters based on the group input.

Tip Write a letter to your class on a subject of current interest to students, such as a planned class outing or a challenging assignment. Challenge students to critique your letter using the questions in the Follow Up above.

Expository Writing

100 Writing Lessons © by Tara McCarthy • Scholastic Teaching Resources

Name _____ Date _____

Audience: CORRESPOND WITH SOMEONE YOU KNOW

Choose a topic from the box below or think of one of your own. Underline the topic or write it on the line below.

> **what relatives are doing**   **what mutual friends are doing**
> **your new hobby or interest**   **what school is like this year**
> **changes in your community**   **a big event in your family**
>
> _____

Now choose the recipient of your letter or think of one of your own. Underline the recipient or write the name on the line below.

> **a classmate who has moved away**   **a relative who lives far away**
> **a family member who is traveling** **a person you met on vacation**
>
> _____

Write a letter about the topic to the recipient you've chosen. Use the other side of this sheet if you need to.

Dear _____ ,

_____

_____

_____

                              All the best,

                              _____

Expository Writing

Audience: WRITE TO SOMEONE YOU DON'T KNOW

> Goal: Write a formal letter on a topic that matters.

➡ Get Set

Read aloud two or three Letters to the Editor on topics of special interest to your students, such as the environment or school safety. Point out that the writers are directing their message to people they may not know personally but whom they want to influence with their opinions. Ask: *Which should be formal and detailed—a letter to the editor or a letter to someone you know well? Why?*

➡ Go

Show the reproducible on page 163 on an overhead. Focus on one of the issues, such as *What shall we do about abandoned pets?* Ask for students' suggestions and use the ideas to fill in the *Points to Make* circles in the web on the reproducible. Here are some points: *Families shouldn't acquire pets unless they're prepared to take care of them. If you suddenly can't take care of your pet, find a good home for it.* Work with students to develop an opening sentence, such as *Along our streets and highways, we see many abandoned cats and dogs that need to be rescued and cared for.*

➡ Follow Up

Hand out the reproducible on page 163. Ask students to choose another issue, complete the web, and draft a letter to the editor on the issue. Remind them that the first sentence should state the issue clearly and then be supported by important points. Encourage students to read aloud their letters and to ask for their classmates' comments and suggestions. Suggest that students submit their revised and edited letters to the local newspaper, as appropriate.

> **Tip** Issue Posters also present core ideas to a large audience. Some students will enjoy the challenge of showing the issue and the points graphically in a poster instead of a letter.

Expository Writing

Name _____ Date _____

Audience: WRITE TO SOMEONE YOU DON'T KNOW

Choose one of the issues below or write another issue you would like to develop on the line below instead.

> **What shall we do about abandoned pets?**
> **How can we expand our after-school or sports program?**
> **Is it fair to have some students repeat a grade?**
> **Do violent TV programs encourage real-life violence?**
>
> _____

Copy the web on a separate sheet of paper. Write your issue in the center circle in the web. Write the important points you want to make in the surrounding circles.

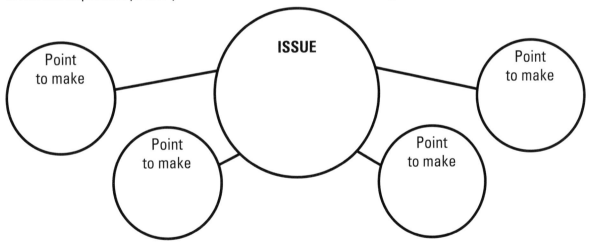

Now draft a letter to the editor on the issue. Write your opening sentence on the line below. Use the important points to develop your letter. You can write on the back of this sheet if you need to.

To the Editor: _____

_____

_____

Expository Writing

Audience: HOOK YOUR AUDIENCE!

> Goal: Write an engaging opening sentence.

➡ Get Set

On the board, write the following pairs of sample opening sentences for a report. Ask students which sentences are the best attention-grabbers and why.

- My report is about newts.
  A tiny orange lizard-like thing scurried by me!
- This report is about stars.
  Wow! What a gleaming display is in the clear night sky!
- Here's what I've found out about advertisers.
  Don't believe everything you see and hear.

Point out that the second sentence in each pair piques readers' curiosity and makes them want to read on.

➡ Go

Distribute the reproducible on page 165. Suggest some entries students might write in the Topic column (e.g., a field trip, a class play, a craft fair to raise money for a student travel-abroad program). Then ask students—working independently or in pairs—to write catchy, engaging opening sentences for the "billboards." For example, a billboard about raising money for the travel-abroad program might read "Please send us away!"

➡ Follow Up

Invite students to read aloud their billboard openers to the class. Talk about which openers hooked the audience and why they did.

> **Tip** Ask students to write opening sentences for advertisements for ordinary classroom objects, such as the chalkboard or whiteboard, student desks, pencils, or bulletin boards. You might provide examples like these:
>
> - Sit on it! Move it! Enjoy the four-legged classroom wonder! (chair)
> - You'll laugh when you meet the newest members of our class! (gerbils in cages)
>
> After sharing the openers, discuss what's catchy and inviting about them.

Expository Writing

Name _____ Date _____

Audience: HOOK YOUR AUDIENCE!

Write topics on the left. Then write attention-grabbing opening sentences on the billboards on the right.

1. Topic: _____

2. Topic: _____

3. Topic: _____

Expository Writing

On the board or overhead, display the chart below.

TOPIC	AUDIENCE
bears	adults at home
traffic hazards	little kids
good TV shows	your classmates
healthy meals	someone you don't personally know
career choices	just yourself

Discuss how a writer would write about a topic in different ways, depending on the intended audience. Then suggest one of the topics and two different audiences. Supply an opening sentence and one or two additional sentences. Encourage students to complete the paragraphs orally. See the examples below.

Topic: Career Choices

Audience: adults at home
In school, I'm getting some ideas about the various employment opportunities I might have after I graduate from high school. I'm really excited about a couple of them and hope you'll support me as I ...

Audience: little kids
What do you want to do when you grow up? Maybe you're really good at art or music. You could become a painter or a singer. If you work really hard, you can...

Ask partners to choose a topic from the box above. Tell each partner to select a different audience to address on this topic. Allow time for partners to share their writing, discussing how and why their approaches differ and suggesting changes to each other's work.

Expository Writing

Presentation:

GIVE DIRECTIONS TWO WAYS

Goal: Show visually how to go from one place to another and then write the instructions.

➡ Get Set

Distribute the reproducible on page 168. Review the direction to draw a route on the map and write instructions for the route. Discuss which approach students think will be more challenging—drawing the route or describing it in words. (Many kids will say the written approach is more difficult because they will have to be precise in choosing their words.)

➡ Go

Have students work independently to complete the reproducible and then share their work with a partner to compare and discuss the results. Tell partners to decide which route is the easiest and most efficient and then refine their instructions. Ask them to read aloud their instructions as their classmates listen and follow the route on the map. Find out what the rest of the class thinks about the clarity and precision of the instructions.

➡ Follow Up

Recap the guidelines for written directions: Be brief. Be precise. Ask partners to grade themselves from A to C on how well they fulfilled the guidelines.

Tip With students who need practice with or a review of English spatial terms, adapt the old game of Hot and Cold. Hide an ordinary classroom object, such as a pen or a lunchbox. Reveal the name of the object and then use the following phrases to guide students as they search for it:

Go back.	Retrace your steps.	Turn around.
Go forward.	Turn left.	Look to your left.
Look up.	Turn right.	Look to your right.
Look down.	You're near.	You're far away.

Expository Writing

Name _____ Date _____

Presentation:

GIVE DIRECTIONS TWO WAYS

A. Draw lines on the map below to show an easy and efficient route from the Petting Zoo to the Land of Lost Socks.

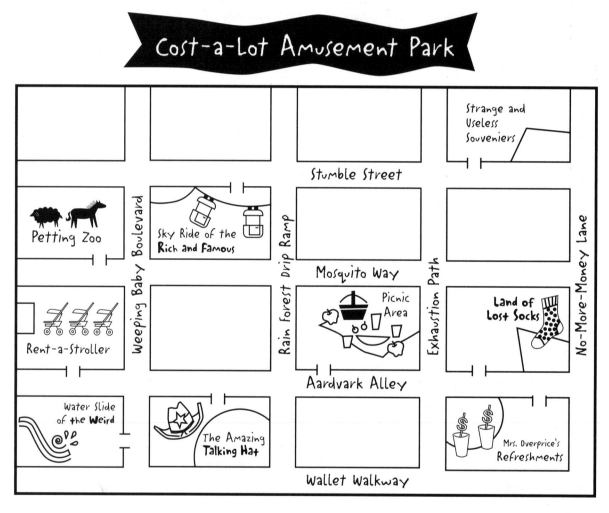

B. Now, on a separate sheet of paper, write instructions for following the route you drew. Use directional words—*north, south, east, west*—and other positional words—*left, right, after, past,* and so on. Be sure to refer to landmarks and street names. And remember: Be brief. Be precise.

Expository Writing

Presentation: GO STEP BY STEP

> Goal: List the steps for carrying out a procedure in order.

➡ Get Set

Hand out the reproducible on page 170 and discuss the steps in playing the game of Find the Mistake. Allow time for groups of five or six students to play the game. Then talk about how the instructions helped them play the game. Question whether they would add to, delete, or change any of the steps, and to explain their thinking.

➡ Go

Distribute the reproducible on page 171. Tell students to work individually or in pairs to write the steps for doing one of their favorite activities.

➡ Follow Up

Ask students to read aloud the steps in their activity to the rest of the class. Gauge the audience's response with questions such as these: *Is the goal clear? Are the steps in order? Are all the steps necessary? Were any steps missing? What suggestions do you have for clarifying the instructions?*

> **Tip** Talk about a TV game show that students are familiar with, such as *Are You Smarter Than a Fifth Grader?* or *Jeopardy.* What are the rules for playing the game? Ask kids to list these rules in numerical order.

Expository Writing

Name _____ Date _____

Presentation: GO STEP BY STEP

A. Here are the rules for playing the game Find the Mistake.

Step 1: Five or six people can play at one time. Each player needs some index cards and a pencil.

Step 2: Each player numbers the card from 1 to 4 and writes four statements about a topic on it. Three of the statements should be true and one should be false. The player writes the false statement on the back of the card.

---

1. Kangaroos are native to Australia.
2. Kangaroos are a kind of amphibian.
3. Kangaroos carry their babies in their pouches.
4. Kangaroos can jump vast distances in one bound.

---

2. Kangaroos are a kind of amphibian.

Step 3: The player holds up the four-statement side of the card and asks the other players to identify the statement that is not true. The first player to do so wins a point.

Step 4: The student who guessed correctly goes next. Whoever scores the most points wins the game.

B. Get together with four or five other classmates.
Follow the above steps to play Find the Mistake.

100 Writing Lessons © by Tara McCarthy • Scholastic Teaching Resources

Expository Writing

Name _____ Date _____

Presentation: GO STEP BY STEP

Think about an activity you know a lot about, such as playing a certain game, painting a portrait of a friend, training a puppy, or finding Web sites that can help you with homework assignments.

Write the steps for completing this activity in order on the lines below. If necessary, you can add more steps or delete some.

Steps for _____

1. _____

_____

_____

2. _____

_____

_____

3. _____

_____

_____

4. _____

_____

_____

5. _____

_____

_____

Expository Writing

Expository Writing

Presentation: DESIGN AN INVITATION

> Goal: Provide essential facts in a limited amount of space.

➡Get Set

Ask students to imagine they're sending out invitations to a birthday party. Hold up a postcard. Explain the challenge of the activity: All the information about the party has to be contained within this small space. Ask students what their invited guests have to know. Emphasize the following elements: *Who the party is for; when and where the party will take place; how to get there; what special things the guests should prepare for.* With student input, create and complete the postcard invitation below.

➡Go

Distribute the reproducible on page 173. Ask students to read the instructions and carry out the activity independently.

➡Follow Up

Call on students to read aloud their invitations. Have classmates listen and pay attention to whether the invitation contains all the vital information or if there is additional information they'd like to know about the event.

Tip Use a concept-through-contrast approach. Write the following invitation on the board:
Come to our Laugh-In party! Lots of fun for everyone! Practice your favorite jokes and imitations to share with all of us!
Ask students what information is missing from the invitation. As they supply the information, write it on the invitation.

Expository Writing

Name _____ Date _____

Presentation: DESIGN AN INVITATION

A. Circle an occasion in the box below or think of something else to celebrate.

- You just had braces removed from your teeth.
- You won a million dollars in the lottery.
- Your essay won first prize in the school-wide contest.
- Your dog won first prize in the kennel show.
- Your teacher said you're so smart that you don't need to attend school anymore.

B. Write the important information for your invitation on the postcard. Be brief!

WHO THE PARTY IS FOR

_____

WHAT YOU'RE CELEBRATING

_____

WHEN YOU'RE CELEBRATING

_____

WHERE YOU'RE CELEBRATING

_____

HOW TO GET THERE

_____

SPECIAL NOTE

_____

_____
_____
_____

USA FIRST-CLASS FOREVER

100 Writing Lessons © by Tara McCarthy • Scholastic Teaching Resources

Expository Writing

Presentation: TRY AN INTERVIEW

> Goal: Develop a topic by asking and answering specific questions.

➡ Get Set

Briefly discuss TV talk shows, like Oprah Winfrey's, where the host asks interesting questions related to a specific facet of the guest's life, such as a special goal or achievement. Then ask students to imagine that they could interview anyone in the world from now or the past. What particular aspect of the interviewee's life would they focus on? What are some questions they would ask? Remind students that most good questions are W-H questions (who, what, when, where, why, how), and that they should avoid questions that can be answered with only a "yes" or a "no."

Write some of the students' suggestions on the board.

> An Interview with . . .
> - Queen Nerfertiti • Frederick Douglass • Tiger Woods
> - Christopher Columbus • Sally Ride

➡ Go

Distribute the reproducible on page 175. Have student interviewers write their questions on the sheet and then exchange them with their partners. Allow time for student interviewees to assume the role of the important person and respond to the questions. Then tell partners to read aloud their questions and responses, editing and revising as they discuss the interview.

➡ Follow Up

Ask partners to read aloud their interview scripts to the class. Remind the audience to listen for the W-H questions that evoke the most interesting responses.

Tip Cut out photos—minus the captions—from newspapers and magazines that show people involved in interesting situations. Challenge students to ask W-H questions about the situation as if they were addressing the individuals shown. Record kids' questions and invite other students to respond as if they were the pictured individuals. (This activity can be as serious or as playful as you care to make it.)

Expository Writing

Name _____ Date _____

Presentation: TRY AN INTERVIEW

Write the name of an important person—from the past or the present—whom you would like to interview.

My interview with

_____

Now write your interview questions. Your partner will assume the role of the person and answer the questions, and vice versa.

Question 1: _____

_____

Answer: _____

_____

Question 2: _____

_____

Answer: _____

_____

Question 3: _____

_____

Answer: _____

_____

Question 4: _____

_____

Answer: _____

_____

Question 5: _____

_____

Answer: _____

_____

Expository Writing

Presentation: ORGANIZE YOUR IDEAS

Goal: Plan how to develop a topic in order to present it.

➡ Get Set

On the overhead, show the graphic organizer on page 177. With students, choose a topic and work together to fill in the organizer. (See the example below.) Review the following elements of expository writing as you proceed:

- The first paragraph begins by stating the main idea and then begins to develop the first main points or examples.
- The second paragraph presents and develops the other main points or examples.
- The third paragraph presents final examples. It ends by restating and summarizing the main idea.

My Topic: Detecting Misleading Advertisements
Paragraph 1 Lead Sentence If you're like most people, you've fallen for ads that promise but don't deliver.
Examples, Points 1. popularity 2. good looks   3. better health

Paragraph 2 Lead Sentence Now, however, you've learned to detect advertisers' pitches to special audiences.
Examples, Points 1. little kids 2. people in debt 3. people who want to be the first to have something

Paragraph 3 Lead Sentence You get to recognize how ads can mislead you.
Examples, Points 1. show things larger 2. claim that a famous star uses the product
3. hurry or you'll miss your chance

Summary: All in all, advertisements can be misleading by making big promises, appealing to your weaknesses, and piquing your interest with unrealistic pictures, a sense of urgency, and celebrity testimonials.

➡ Go

Distribute the reproducible on page 177. Ask partners to choose another topic from the list and use the graphic organizer to develop it.

➡ Follow Up

Invite partners to write the first draft of a three-paragraph essay based on the data in their graphic organizer. Stress that this is purely for practice! But also suggest that partners might want to share their draft with a larger group to get feedback for a second draft.

Tip You may want to carry out the Follow Up activity by working with a small group of students to develop a three-paragraph expository essay based on the topic and model you presented in the Get Set section. Students can add or delete ideas for the essay while you act as scribe at the board. They will also learn a lot as they watch you punctuate and indent paragraphs appropriately. Bring the activity to a close (and instill a sense of accomplishment) by asking each student to write a copy of the final draft.

Expository Writing

Name _____ Date _____

Presentation: ORGANIZE YOUR IDEAS

A. Circle the topic below that you would like to develop.

> **Misleading Ads**   **School Fads**   **Hints for New Students**
>
> **Everyday Hazards at Home and at School**   **The Best Movie of the Year**

B. Use the graphic organizer to help you develop the topic and then present it.

My Topic: _____

| **Paragraph 1**
 Lead Sentence
 ↓
 Examples, Points
 1._____
 _____
 2._____
 _____
 3._____
 _____ | **Paragraph 2**
 Lead Sentence
 ↓
 Examples, Points
 1._____
 _____
 2._____
 _____
 3._____
 _____ | **Paragraph 3**
 Lead Sentence
 ↓
 Examples, Points
 1._____
 _____
 2._____
 _____
 3._____
 _____ |

↓

Summary: _____

_____

_____

_____

_____

Presentation: WIND-UP

Expository writing implies an audience for one's ideas. Encourage students to edit and revise any one of the writing activities they've done in this section and then to read the finished product aloud to the entire class. Acknowledge that an all-by-yourself-in-front-of-the-whole-class-reading can sound like a scary assignment but that it's also a great ego-booster to share your best expository work with a big audience. Suggest the following sequential steps and/or make copies of them for students:

1. Read your work aloud to yourself. Make corrections in your writing, where needed. Underline important phrases and sentences that you'll want to stress as you read them aloud.

2. Practice by reading your piece to a very small test audience of four or five classmates. Speak more slowly than you would in ordinary conversation. Get feedback on this oral presentation.

3. Look up at your audience now and then as you read. If you have practiced and know your own writing well, this can be easy to do.

4. Act it out or show it. Use visuals or charts to help make your points. The more you can move around and point to things, the more comfortable you'll feel.

5. If you're still suffering from stage fright, use a round-table approach. Put a table in front of the class and have four or five classmates sit around it. Read aloud your work to these classmates, but speak loud enough for everyone in the room to hear you.

Expository Writing

Name _____ Date _____

On Your Own:
EXPLAIN YOUR ROUTINE IN A POEM

Now and then, cowboy poets get together to share the poems they've written about their work.
Here's an example that gives a step-by-step account of one cowboy's routine:

You herd the cattle,
Stop for the night,
Cook your grub and stare at the stars.
A lonely life.
Next day, you're up and at it again.
Delivery done, you head back home.
Miles and miles of lonely miles to go.
Would you give it up, this life?
No way!

Write a step-by-step poem about a routine you follow in your everyday life.

_____

_____

_____

_____

_____

_____

_____

_____

_____

_____

Expository Writing

Name _____ Date _____

On Your Own:
GIVE TIPS TO AMAZING NEW STUDENTS

A character in a book you know well enters your classroom as a new student. List steps that could help him or her adjust. Study the example below.

New Student: **Winnie the Pooh**
Steps: **1.** Don't count on Christopher Robin being here to help you.
         2. Ask me about ways to avoid bees' nests.
         3. Try the school diet lunch in order to lose weight.
         4. Pay no attention to mean students who mock you for being a bear.

New Student: _____

1. _____

_____

_____

2. _____

_____

_____

3. _____

_____

_____

4. _____

_____

_____

100 Writing Lessons © by Tara McCarthy • Scholastic Teaching Resources

Expository Writing

Name _____ Date _____

On Your Own: DEFINE NEW WORDS

New words enter our language every day. Here are two we've just made up and defined.

> **flumtatious** *adj.* describes how someone exaggerates his or her achievements:
> *She was flumtatious about her performance in the marathon.*
>
> **oversnooze** *n.* a nap that goes on too long: *Because of his oversnooze,*
> *he missed the start of the marathon.*

Write your own definitions and examples for the new words below.

1. musicflop *n.* _____

_____

_____

2. floop *v.* _____

_____

_____

3. throwopic *adj.* _____

_____

_____

4. plunkify *v.* _____

_____

_____

5. bwiddle *n.* _____

_____

_____

Expository Writing

Name _____ Date _____

On Your Own: WHO DID THAT?

Nobody really knows who invented the items listed in the box below. Pretend that you have discovered the facts and history behind the invention of one item. Write one or two expository paragraphs that tell about the inventor and how she or he created this wonderful item.

shoelaces	hats	dishes	tables
dancing	schools	music	swings

_____

_____

_____

_____

_____

_____

_____

_____

_____

_____

_____

_____

_____

_____

_____

_____

100 Writing Lessons © by Tara McCarthy • Scholastic Teaching Resources

Expository Writing

Name _____ Date _____

On Your Own:
REPORT AN UNUSUAL EVENT

Imagine that you're a newspaper reporter. Your assignment: Get the facts about the strange case of Dr. Fluster. The poor fellow was trapped in a huge parking garage for two days because he couldn't find the exit! Now that he's been rescued, he's ready for you to interview him. Write your Who-What-When-Why-Where-How questions on the lines below. Make brief notes about Dr. Fluster's answers.

YOUR QUESTIONS   **THE DOCTOR'S ANSWERS**

1. Who?

_____   _____

_____   _____

2. What?

_____   _____

_____   _____

3. When?

_____   _____

_____   _____

4. Where?

_____   _____

_____   _____

5. Why?

_____   _____

_____   _____

6. How?

_____   _____

_____   _____

On the back of this sheet or another sheet of paper, draft a news report using the facts you've collected.

Expository Writing

Expository Writing

100 Writing Lessons © by Tara McCarthy • Scholastic Teaching Resources

Name _____ Date _____

On Your Own: RATE YOURSELF

1. For you, what's the most challenging or hardest thing about expository writing?

_____

_____

_____

_____

2. For you, what's the easiest thing about expository writing?

_____

_____

_____

_____

3. Of all the expository writing you've done in this section, which piece pleases you the most? Why?

_____

_____

_____

_____

4. Of all the expository writing you've done in this section, which pleases you the least? Why?

_____

_____

_____

_____

Persuasive Writing

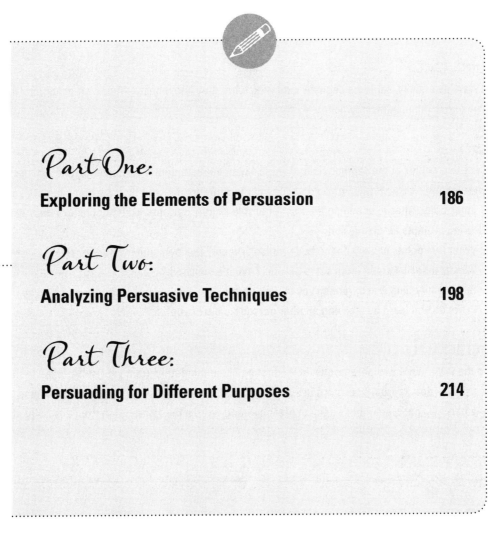

Persuasive Writing

Exploring the Elements of Persuasion:
STATING OPINIONS

> Goal: Exploring different points of view.

➡ Get Set

In this start-up activity, students begin by exploring what they know best—their own opinions. Then they expand their thinking to include the viewpoints of others.

➡ Go

Distribute two copies of the reproducible on page 187 to each student. Pair students, and ask each partner to list his or her talents and best qualities on one copy of the reproducible and their partner's talents and best qualities on the other copy. After exchanging their set of profile pages, partners skim to compare their opinions. Suggest the following prompts for discussion:

- What two points of view do the two profiles present? (my own and my partner's)
- What's different about each set of profiles? What's the same?
- Is there anything that surprises you in your partner's profile of you? Is there anything you disagree with?
- What do you learn by studying another person's view of you?

➡ Follow Up

Explain the task: Write two paragraphs. In the first one, use the details from your self-profile. In the second paragraph, use the details from your partner's profile of you. Then encourage students to imagine a third point of view—a parent's, pet's, neighbor's opinion of them—and write a third paragraph from this point of view.

> **Tip** Suggest a title for the paragraphs, such as "All About Me," and a topic sentence for each paragraph that identifies the point of view: *Here is how I see myself. Here is my partner's view of me. I'm Lucinda's dog, Muffin, and here's my view of Lucinda.*

Persuasive Writing

Name _____ Date _____

Exploring the Elements of Persuasion: STATING OPINIONS

This is my profile of _____

Talents and Best Qualities

_____

_____

_____

_____

_____

_____

_____

_____

Persuasive Writing

Exploring the Elements of Persuasion:
USING SUPPORTING FACTS AND EXAMPLES

> **Goal:** Distinguish between fact and opinion.

➡ Get Set

Distinguishing between fact and opinion can be a rigorous cognitive task for writers and readers of all ages. Ask students to use dictionaries and thesauruses to find and share definitions of the word *fact*. Present some simple examples of facts from your science or geography curriculum: *Mexico is south of the United States. The sun rises in the east and sets in the west.*

➡ Go

Ask students for other statements of fact they've learned in science or geography and list them on the board. Encourage questioning: If students are not sure that a classmate's statement is a fact, write *Show Me!* after it. Ask: *What more would you have to know before you accepted this statement as fact?* (more facts, an explanation, examples, proof)

➡ Follow Up

Refer students to the partner profiles they made in the previous lesson (pp. 186–187). After distributing the reproducible on page 189, tell them to choose one profile item (for example, Lucinda helps other kids) and write it under Fact in the Fact-Example Cluster. If the statement is a fact, then students will be able to complete the cluster with supporting examples. Have them use the Fact-Example Cluster as a guideline to draft a persuasive paragraph.

Tip Suggest the following format for the persuasive paragraph:
- Sentence 1: State the fact at the center of the cluster.
- Sentences 2, 3, 4, 5 . . . : State the supporting examples.
- Final Sentence: State how your fact is supported by the examples.

Persuasive Writing

Name _____ Date _____

Exploring the Elements of Persuasion: USING SUPPORTING FACTS AND EXAMPLES

A. Use the profiles you created in the lesson on Stating Opinions (pp. 186–187) to fill in this Fact-Example Cluster. Choose one fact and write it in the center. Write examples to support that fact in the outside boxes.

Fact-Example Cluster

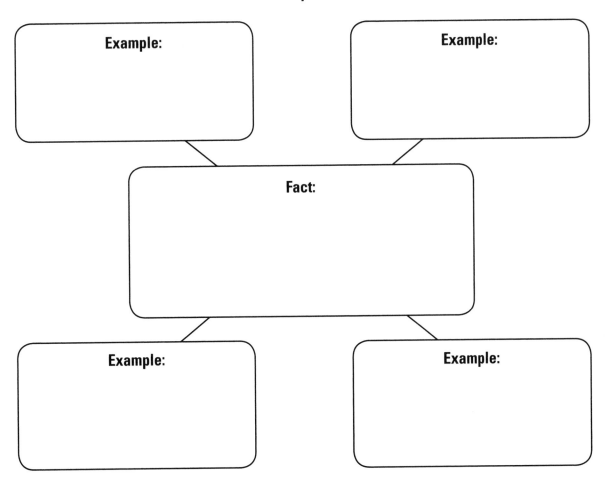

B. Now, use the cluster to help you write a persuasive paragraph centered around the fact.

Persuasive Writing

Exploring the Elements of Persuasion:
LOGIC AND REASONING

Goal: Show how a logical argument presents related ideas in sequence.

➡ Get Set

Hand out copies of the reproducible on page 191. Explain that the first sentence in Paragraph A states the writer's opinion, but that the other sentences are out of order: that is, they don't follow a logical sequence. Read aloud the paragraph to the class and discuss how to reorder sentences 2–5 so one idea leads logically to the next.

➡ Go

Focus on Paragraph B. Call attention to the opening and concluding sentences, and invite students to identify the writer's opinion on the subject of school lunches from those sentences. Then ask them to reread the paragraph and think about the two sentences that don't have anything to do with the writer's point of view. (Sentences 4 and 7)

➡ Follow Up

Have students work independently to rewrite the paragraph, deleting the unnecessary sentences. Then group students so they can discuss their decisions and rewrites.

Tip An example of how to reorder the sentences in Paragraph A is 1, 3, 5, 2, 4. However, students may suggest a different order—and that's fine. The objective here is to simply get kids focused on the importance of presenting an argument through steps the audience can easily follow.

Persuasive Writing

Name _____ Date _____

Exploring the Elements of Persuasion:
LOGIC AND REASONING

A. Read Paragraph A. On a separate sheet of paper, reorder the sentences so they are in logical order.

> **Paragraph A**
> (1) Animal shelters are overcrowded because many pet owners are irresponsible. (2) They bring these animals to the shelter. (3) For example, a family may buy a cat or dog without thinking ahead of time about the care the animal requires. (4) Many abandoned pets have to be put to sleep there because of the thoughtlessness of their original owners. (5) Or the owner may fail to get the pet neutered and then become upset by an unwelcome litter of kittens or puppies.

B. Read Paragraph B. Which sentences are unnecessary? On a separate sheet of paper, rewrite the paragraph, deleting those sentences.

> (1) Kids want a lot of choices at lunchtime. (2) The cafeteria cooks do a good job of appealing to kids who want a really well-balanced meal. (3) But some kids just want snacks like the ones that BurgerBelly sells—snacks like Potato Puffies, BabyBurgs, and Icey-Ikes. (4) My parents always buy a sack of Potato Puffies to eat at the movies. (5) Our school should make both kinds of meals available. (6) Let's persuade our local BurgerBelly to sell food at lunchtime in our cafeteria. (7) BurgerBelly was founded by R. U. Hungry of Portly, Arkansas. (8) Then we would all be able to choose between cafeteria meals and fast-food snacks.

Persuasive Writing

Exploring the Elements of Persuasion:
JUST LISTEN TO THAT!

> **Goal:** Assess the persuasive skills of debate participants.

➡ **Get Set**

Show brief video clips of an election debate or discussion program on television.

➡ **Go**

Discuss the debate or discussion program with students. Prompt discussion with questions, such as *What makes an argument helpful to someone who wants to know all about an issue? What makes an argument confusing, distracting, or incomplete? How would you rate the speakers you just saw?* Then distribute the reproducible on page 193 and work with students in completing it.

➡ **Follow Up**

Hand out another copy of the same reproducible. Ask students to watch a discussion or debate at home with their families and get their family member's input in completing the reproducible.

You may want to challenge students who saw the same program to reenact it for the class. Ask them to think about how they could improve the arguments by making the topic, points of view, and supporting details clearer and by correcting any bad behavior, such as interrupting, making faces, and calling people names.

Tip You may want to bring in a TV schedule and have students scan it to determine which programs they'll watch at home. Also, compose a note to send home with students that explains the task to their families.

Persuasive Writing

Name _____ Date _____

Exploring the Elements of Persuasion:
JUST LISTEN TO THAT!

Name of Program I Watched: _____

Date: _____ **Time:** _____ **Channel:** _____

Participants	Their Titles, Jobs, or Backgrounds
_____	_____
_____	_____
_____	_____
_____	_____
_____	_____

What was the Big Issue that the speakers discussed?

_____

_____

_____

Grade the participants:

- **Who was best at sticking to the point?** _____
- **Who was vague or said things that didn't have anything to do with the issue?**

_____

- **Did any of the participants have "bad manners" such as interrupting, making faces, or attacking the personality of an opponent? If so, give an example.**

_____

_____

What was the most important thing you learned about . . .

- **the issue that the speakers were debating?** _____
- **how to (or how not to) present opinions?** _____

100 Writing Lessons © by Tara McCarthy • Scholastic Teaching Resources

Persuasive Writing

Exploring the Elements of Persuasion:
THINKING ABOUT YOUR AUDIENCE

Goal: Explore how to change the audience's mind.

➡ Get Set

One goal of persuasive writing is to bring an undecided audience around to the writer's point of view. A second goal of the writer—more difficult to achieve—is to convince an audience with an opinion contrary to the writer's to switch sides. In the latter case, the writer's first step is to understand why the target audience holds the opinion.

➡ Go

Remind students that writers who want to persuade audiences to accept a particular point of view need to remember that different people may look at the same situation in different ways.

Distribute the reproducible on page 195 and preview the task and directions. Work with the class in completing Part 1, listing the pros and cons of having snack and soda machines in the school cafeteria.

➡ Follow Up

Discuss what it means to be objective: to consider all the ideas that relate to a situation, regardless of your personal opinions. Ask pairs to work together to complete Part 2 of the reproducible. Then challenge them to use their lists to develop a persuasive paragraph presenting the YES and NO sides.

Tip Establish the following guidelines for the persuasive paragraphs:
- The topic sentence rewords the original question to make it a statement.
- The follow-up sentences state the pros and cons objectively.

Persuasive Writing

Name _____ Date _____

Exploring the Elements of Persuasion:
THINKING ABOUT YOUR AUDIENCE

ANALYZING DIFFERENT VIEWPOINTS

Part 1: Students in one school are debating this issue:

Should our school cafeteria have snack and soda machines in the cafeteria?

Some students say "Yes." Some students say "No."

List some reasons to support each side of the debate.

YES Reasons: **NO Reasons:**

_____ _____

_____ _____

_____ _____

_____ _____

_____ _____

_____ _____

Part 2: Choose one of the questions below. On a separate sheet of paper, list reasons to support **YES** answers and reasons to support **NO** answers. Strive for the same number of reasons in each list.

- Should our school have a no-homework policy?
- Should every student be required to learn a foreign language?
- Should students in our school wear uniforms?
- Should students repeat a grade if they don't pass final tests?
- Should students be able to skip a grade if their schoolwork is outstanding?

Persuasive Writing

Exploring the Elements of Persuasion: WIND-UP

Gather several periodical articles that detail the views of opposing factions on an issue (e.g., developers vs. environmentalists, groups that want more tax money to go to school vs. groups that don't, Democrats vs. Republicans). Distribute the different articles to groups of four or five students.

Explain the activity:

- read the article
- determine the issue (what the argument is about)
- determine the different points of view
- write a paragraph summarizing the viewpoints, using the following format:
    + 1st sentence: State what the issue is about.
    + 2nd sentence: Identify the groups that are debating the issue.
    + 3rd sentence: Summarize the point of view of one group.
    + 4th sentence: Summarize the point of view of the other group.

Ask each group to appoint a spokesperson to read the group's paragraph to the class. The audience listens to determine if the speakers present their contentions clearly. A larger question for the audience is, *Has the group managed in its paragraph to be objective, that is, to not take sides?* Groups may wish to revise their paragraphs on the basis of class comments.

Name _____ Date _____

 Exploring the Elements of Persuasion:
WIND-UP

After everyone in your group reads the article your teacher passed out, do the following:

- determine the issue (what the argument is about) in the article
- determine the different points of view in the article
- write a paragraph summarizing those viewpoints, using the following format:
    + 1st sentence: State what the issue is about.
    + 2nd sentence: Identify the groups that are debating the issue.
    + 3rd sentence: Summarize the point of view of one group.
    + 4th sentence: Summarize the point of view of the other group.

Here's an example:

EXAMPLE

The issue is whether a nuclear power plant should be built on the shore of the Tumble River. The parties discussing the issue are the PowerCenter Corporation and Citizens for Safety. The point of view of the PowerCenter Corporation is that a nuclear power plant would supply customers with inexpensive electric power. The point of view of Citizens for Safety is that nuclear power plants can have accidents that threaten human health.

---

100 Writing Lessons © by Tara McCarthy • Scholastic Teaching Resources

Persuasive Writing

Analyzing Persuasive Techniques:
GET ON THE BANDWAGON!

> Goal: Examine persuasive techniques used in advertising.

➡ Get Set

Begin by telling students what a *bandwagon* is: a highly decorated parade float crowded with enthusiastic participants in an event (for example, clowns, musicians, political figures).

Then write the following statements on the board—without the underlining; students will do that.

- Get into jeans with the Glow! <u>Up-to-date</u> kids proudly wear the Glow Jeans glow-stripe day and night!
- <u>Everyone</u> is collecting them! Are you? Buy the latest Fluffy Friend before <u>millions of collectors</u> buy out the entire supply!
- What's the <u>favorite</u> after-school snack? <u>Nine-out-of-ten kids</u> rush home to gobble up the all-time, all-around winner, Sniggle Bars.
- <u>People-in-the-know</u> are switching to Pasta-Paste, the toothpaste that hundreds of dentists recommend because it tastes like spaghetti.

➡ Go

Ask students to read the statements and identify the bandwagon words and phrases. Call on volunteers to underline the words and phrases that classmates identify. Then initiate a lively debate of the issues raised by the language.

➡ Follow Up

Hand out copies of reproducibles on page 199. Have the class brainstorm a list of generic items and write them on the board. Tell students to choose an item, give it an original brand name—for example, Leap 'n' Stride for a pair of sneakers—and write an ad that uses the bandwagon technique of persuasion.

Tip Use prompts such as these to spark discussion: *How do the words and phrases make the audience feel that they absolutely must buy the product? Is a product that's a best-seller necessarily better than a product that isn't as popular? What's a fad? What are the advantages and disadvantages of getting on the bandwagon? What details—if any—are supplied to show the source of language such as "everyone," "people in the know," "nine-out-of-ten," and so on?*

Persuasive Writing

Name _____ Date _____

Analyzing Persuasive Techniques:
GET ON THE BANDWAGON!

Choose an item from the list your class brainstormed. Give the item an original brand name and write an ad that uses the bandwagon technique of persuasion.

The best advertizing in town!
Place classified ads at adsales.com

Persuasive Writing

Analyzing Persuasive Techniques:
TESTIMONIALS–
THE FAMOUS-PEOPLE TECHNIQUE

Goal: Analyze ads that feature famous people.

➡ Get Set

Almost every student will be able to come up with examples of TV commercials that feature a famous person—for example, sports stars speaking for makers of sporting goods; TV and movie actors featured in ads for clothing and perfume.

➡ Go

Ask the class to name some products or services that use a famous spokesperson to testify to the supposed greatness of the product or service. List students' examples on the board, and then pose the following questions:

- Why do advertisers use famous people in ad campaigns? (The audience admires superstars and thinks, "If she/he says it's good, it must be!"
- In which ads might the spokesperson actually be an expert in the kind of product advertised? (A basketball player might know a lot about athletic shoes.) In which ads is the spokesperson unlikely to know a great deal about the product or service? (A TV actor might not know much more than the rest of us about competing telephone services.)
- What's the usual reason that famous people act as spokespeople for a product or service? (They get paid for doing so.)
- Sometimes famous people donate their time for free for a charitable cause, such as feeding the hungry or fighting a specific disease. Why might they donate their time for this kind of work? (They truly believe in the cause; they want all the money to go to the cause and not to pay a spokesperson.)

➡ Follow Up

Distribute the reproducible on page 201, and have students create their own testimonials for famous spokespeople to deliver.

Tip Suggest that students read aloud the drafts of their testimonial speeches to a small group of classmates to determine how persuasive their spokesperson is.

Name _____ Date _____

Analyzing Persuasive Techniques:
TESTIMONIALS–
THE FAMOUS-PEOPLE TECHNIQUE

Now it's your turn to write a testimonial for a product, service, or charity you want the audience to buy or support. Follow these steps:

- Choose a product or service you want to sell or a charity you want to support. The product or service can be real or one that you created for the bandwagon activity on page 198–199.

_____

- Decide on a real-life superstar to be a spokesperson for your company or cause. Why would this person be especially effective in persuading people?

_____

_____

- Write a short testimonial speech for the spokesperson to share with the audience. The speech might open with an identifying lead-in—for example, "You probably recognize me as the eight-time winner of the All-Star trophy." Use some bandwagon words and phrases in the testimonial.

100 Writing Lessons © by Tara McCarthy • Scholastic Teaching Resources

Persuasive Writing

Analyzing Persuasive Techniques:

GLITTERING GENERALITIES

Goal: Use logic and critical-thinking skills to identify persuasive language in ads.

➡ Get Set

This activity not only helps students recognize vague, general terms but also encourages them to be specific in their own writing and speaking.

➡ Go

Hand out a copy of the reproducible on page 203 and go over the definitions of *generality* and *glittering generality* with students. Then challenge them to use logical and critical-thinking skills to come up with questions that a savvy consumer might ask upon hearing or reading an ad that contains each of the glittering generalities in the chart on the reproducible.

Work with the class to rewrite one of the ads in Section B of the reproducible to make the persuasive language more specific. (Example: *We've improved Tooth-Saver by placing the bristles so that they really slant in on those hard-to-reach spots. This new design can help you remove plaque from all your teeth!*)

➡ Follow Up

Ask students to work independently or with a partner to write an original ad that backs up its glittering generalities with specific details.

Tip Bring in a variety of materials for students to study to get ideas for their original ads, including catalogs, flyers, magazines, newspapers, and videotaped TV commercials.

Persuasive Writing

Name _____ Date _____

Analyzing Persuasive Techniques:
GLITTERING GENERALITIES

A. A *generality* is a vague word, phrase, or statement. A *glittering generality* is one that has a feel-good quality to it. What kind of questions should smart consumers ask when they see the following glittering generalities in an ad?

Glittering Generality	Our Questions
better **more powerful** **new, improved** **most popular** **healthy, nutritious** **satisfied customers**	Better than what?

B. Rewrite one of the following ads to make it more specific.

Wild Ranger
more powerful, most popular on the highway!

Chock-O-Mints are the better after-school snack!

New, improved Tooth-Saver!
Buy It Today!

Satisfied customers gobble up healthy, nutritious **Beebee's Breakfast Bonanza Bars!**

C. Now work on your own or with a partner to create an ad or commercial that uses a glittering generality—but that backs it up with specific details.

Persuasive Writing

100 Writing Lessons © by Tara McCarthy • Scholastic Teaching Resources

Persuasive Writing

Analyzing Persuasive Techniques:
TRANSFER-PICTURES AND
SLOGANS THAT PERSUADE

Goal: Realize the persuasive power of visual symbols and catchwords and catchphrases.

➡ Get Set

Ask students to quickly brainstorm what comes to mind when they see the following symbols or read the following catchwords (sample responses appear in parentheses):

- Draw a smiley face. (happiness, fun)
- Write the words, LIMITED SUPPLY! (I better get this fast!)
- Show a photo of the Statue of Liberty. (America, freedom, welcome)
- Write the words: You Are A Winner! (Wow! What did I win?)
- Show a photo of a puppy. (soft and cuddly, a good friend)

Discuss what *transfer* means in persuasive writing: using a strong pictorial symbol or general phrase that arouses the audience's emotions so that they'll connect—transfer—the emotion to the product being sold. Point out that transfer techniques appeal to universal feelings—for example, happiness, fear, patriotism, urgency, wanting to be rich, love of animals. Talk about how the examples in the Get Set section show an appeal to emotions.

➡ Go

Distribute the reproducible on page 205. Divide the class into four or five groups. Give groups time to study the collection of ads you brought in for the previous activity, and then use the ads to complete the chart on the reproducible. You may want to model the first entry for them.

➡ Follow Up

Ask students to work independently or with a partner to write/design an ad for a product or service (print, TV, or a Web site) that tries to appeal to an audience's emotions.

Tip Encourage students not only to create ads for ordinary, realistic goods and services but also to use their imaginations to come up with a bizarre or unusual product or service, such as chocolate-flavored pasta or expeditions to uncomfortable places—e.g., a planet where there is no water.

Persuasive Writing

Name _____ Date _____

Analyzing Persuasive Techniques:
TRANSFER–PICTURES AND SLOGANS THAT PERSUADE

Some persuasive writing, such as advertisements, uses the technique of transfer. The writer uses strong pictures, symbols, and/or catchwords and catchphrases that appeal to reader's emotions. The goal is for the audience to connect—transfer—the emotion to the product being sold.

With your group, study a collection of persuasive ads and commercials. Use them to complete the chart below. Supply a picture, catchword, or catchphrase that the advertisers use to show the emotion in Column 1. Then identify what product or service the advertiser is selling.

Transfer Technique

Feeling, Emotion	Picture or Catchphrase	What the Advertiser Is Selling
1. Wanting to be healthy		
2. Loving your pets		
3. Wanting to be popular and up-to-date		

1) Go an fieldtrip of school
2) Have poster contest

Persuasive Writing

Analyzing Persuasive Techniques:
POSTER PROMOS

> **Goal:** Use visual images as a persuasive technique.

Get Set

Posters, such as public service announcements about smoking, eating healthy food, and buckling your seatbelt, use a strong visual and a catchy slogan to persuade viewers about an issue. Take students on a tour of the school to see how many persuasive posters they can find.

Go

On your return to the classroom, discuss the features that the posters shared, including the following:

- A large, central picture that summarized the opinion or issue visually.
- The most persuasive words and phrases stood out because of the size of the letters, eye-catching color, special lettering, or positioning.
- Persuasive posters are not overloaded with words. Their message is brief.
- The posters are designed to catch the eye of passers-by.

Which posters did students think were the most successful in conveying their message, and why?

Follow Up

Have students create their own persuasive posters. Brainstorm topics they feel strongly about, such as having access to a Web site, wearing school uniforms, conserving energy, voting, and reading books. Encourage students to create a rough draft of their posters on the reproducible on page 207. After conferring with partners, they can create a full-size poster.

Tip Allow ELL students to use their native language on their rough drafts. Supply a translation yourself or ask a student who is fluent in that language to translate. Tell the student to include the slogan in both languages on their final poster.

Persuasive Writing

Name _____ Date _____

Analyzing Persuasive Techniques: POSTER PROMOS

You can create a poster to try to persuade someone about an issue. A successful persuasive poster contains these elements:

- A large, central picture
- Words and phrases that stand out visually
- Brief phrases that catch people's attention

A. Create a rough draft for a persuasive poster.

B. Talk to a partner about your draft. Should you change anything to make it more persuasive? After making changes, draw a full-size poster.

Persuasive Writing

Analyzing Persuasive Techniques:
CARD-STACKING

> **Goal:** Analyze the persuasive technique of card-stacking.

➡ Get Set

Card-stacking means giving the positive side of your own point of view but none of the positive points of your opponent's position. Card-stacking is not only a common advertising strategy but also one that young people use frequently as they argue for something they want.

➡ Go

Distribute the reproducible on page 209 to students. Call on a volunteer to read aloud the paragraph while the other students follow along. Then discuss the questions on the reproducible and define the term *card-stacking*.

➡ Follow Up

Ask students to work alone or with a partner to rewrite the paragraph on the reproducible so it stacks the cards in favor of keeping dogs as pets. Then invite students or pairs to read aloud their rewrites to the class. Are both arguments equally persuasive? Why or why not?

Tip Give students extra practice with this persuasive technique by having groups look for examples of card-stacking in the collection of ads and commercials you've brought in.

Persuasive Writing

Name _____ Date _____

Analyzing Persuasive Techniques:
CARD-STACKING

A. Read the paragraph below.

Residents of the big apartment projects should not be allowed to have dogs. Dogs that are unfriendly or vicious may attack and hurt other people who live in the project and use the open spaces around it. Dogs are also a health hazard because they dirty the grass, playgrounds, and sidewalks. In addition, dogs that bark and whine a lot make it difficult for people in neighboring apartments to sleep and work.

- What is the writer's opinion about apartment residents having dogs as pets?
- How many reasons does the writer provide to support his or her opinion?
- How many reasons does the writer give for the opposite point of view— that residents *should* be allowed to own dogs?

B. Now rewrite the paragraph in which the cards are stacked in favor of residents being allowed to keep dogs.

Persuasive Writing

Persuasive Writing

Analyzing Persuasive Techniques:
THINKING ABOUT YOUR AUDIENCE

> Goal: Recognize the importance of tone in persuasive writing.

➡ Get Set

For persuasive writers, *tone* means the style or manner of expression we use in addressing the target audience. For example, a tone may be informal or formal, playful or serious, somber or hopeful.

➡ Go

Pass out the reproducible on page 210. Define *tone* for students. Ask the class to identify the tone of each TV commercial or ad in column 3 of the first chart—for example, (1) formal, professional tone to appeal to expert doctors; (2) playful, fun tone to appeal to kids who like physical competition.

➡ Follow Up

Have students work independently or with a partner to write two ads for one of the products in the second chart on the reproducible. The tone of their ads should appeal to two different designated audiences. After the writers read aloud their ads, classmates try to identify the tone and probable audience for each one.

> **Tip** To extend students' work with tone and audience, encourage them to look through the classroom collection of ads to identify those designed to appeal to certain audiences—and that use an appropriate tone for doing so.

Persuasive Writing

Name _____ Date _____

Analyzing Persuasive Techniques:
THINKING ABOUT YOUR AUDIENCE

A. In persuasive writing, tone means the style or manner of expression we use in addressing a target audience. Can you identify the tone of each ad in the chart below?

What I'm Selling: Full-O-Life Vitamin Tablets

Audience	Media	Ad Copy
1. Doctors	A magazine that physicians subscribe to	Plubsome Laboratory's years of success show doctors' confidence in our products. Now you will want to suggest our Full-O-Life vitamins to your patients who suffer from Lazy-Osis, Can't-Do-It-Itis, and Couchess-Potato-Itis Syndrome.
2. Kids	TV	Get up and go! Knock 'em dead! Full-O-Life vitamins turn you into a winner! Astound your friends with your bursts of Full-O-Life energy!

B. Choose one of the products below. Write two ads for it. Each ad should have a different tone that appeals to its audience.

Product	Audiences
1. Plaque-Away Tooth Gel	Dentists, kids
2. Seismo Gorgeous (a new car)	Families with kids or drivers who want to be up-to-date
3. Quacky Snacks (snack for parrots)	Parrot owners or parrots
4. Rosy Foam (liquid soap)	Doctors concerned about patients' hygiene or people who want to smell good
5. Bungey Boos (collectible stuffed toys)	Kids who like to collect stuff or relatives wondering what to give as a birthday gift

Analyzing Persuasive Techniques: WIND-UP

Have students carry out this activity at home. After handing out the reproducible on page 213, explain to students that they should watch three different TV commercials with their families to analyze the persuasive techniques in each one. Preview the data on the chart that they should provide.

Ask students to share and compare the data they collected with the rest of the class. Then pose the following questions:

- What were you able to teach your family about persuasive techniques?
- What details and observations did your family pick up that added to your knowledge of persuasive techniques?

Persuasive Writing

Name _____ Date _____

100 Writing Lessons © by Tara McCarthy • Scholastic Teaching Resources

Analyzing Persuasive Techniques: WIND-UP

CRITIQUING COMMERCIALS

	TECHNIQUES USED	CHANNEL/DATE/TIME
Commercial #1 **Product or Service:**		
Commercial #2 **Product or Service:**		
Commercial #3 **Product or Service:**		

Persuasive Writing

Persuasive Writing

Persuading for Different Purposes:
ANALYZE A MODEL

Goal: Learn the guidelines for persuasive writing.

➡ Get Set

Write the following paragraph on the board or reproduce it to show on the overhead:

A Name of Your Own

If you don't like your name, you should have the right to choose a new one. As a child who at birth was named Ebeneezer Carthinottom Pelonious Smithwhithers, I can attest to the importance of this right. If all of us who do not like our names form a committee, we may be able to convince lawmakers to make Name Change a guaranteed right of kids over the age of eight.

➡ Go

Distribute the reproducible on page 215, and go over the guidelines with students. Then read aloud the above paragraph and ask the class to point out how the paragraph adheres to the guidelines.

Point out that the sample paragraph can be followed by one or more paragraphs that develop the subject with supporting ideas and facts. Challenge students to brainstorm some of these. For example: *older people have the right to change their names, so why shouldn't younger people? Your name should express your view of yourself and how you want other people to react to you.*

➡ Follow Up

Ask students to work independently or with a partner to write a persuasive paragraph to open an argument for or against one of the following ideas:

- Weekend curfews for teenagers
- Building a new shopping mall
- Setting up a school dress code
- Students using cell phones in school
- Requiring all students to learn a second language
- Requiring all students to take music and art classes

Tip Remind writers that their paragraphs are opening paragraphs. Supporting ideas and details should be presented in subsequent paragraphs. Some writers might want to get classmates' input about what these follow-up paragraphs might include.

Persuasive Writing

Name _____ Date _____

Persuading for Different Purposes:
ANALYZE A MODEL

Following these guidelines will help your persuasive writing remain clear and focused.

GUIDELINES FOR PERSUASIVE WRITING

S   STATE YOUR **S**UBJECT.

A   KNOW YOUR **A**UDIENCE.

Y   IDENTIFY **Y**OURSELF.

I   KNOW YOUR **I**NTENTION. WHY ARE YOU WRITING?

T   DECIDE ON THE **T**ONE.

Persuasive Writing

Persuasive Writing

Persuading for Different Purposes:
WRITING EDITORIALS AND LETTERS

Goal: Practice using persuasive strategies in addressing a large audience of readers.

➡ Get Set

Bring in a variety of editorials and letters to the editor that have appeared recently in local and national newspapers. (Ideally, you'll find examples that deal with four or five issues important to your students and that present persuasive arguments for different sides of each issue. Group the examples in Subject Folders for students to use later.)

➡ Go

Distribute the reproducible on page 217. Explain that an editorial is a brief essay written by the editor of a newspaper to express the point of view of the newspaper's management—which is why the writer uses *we* rather than *I*. After you read aloud the editorial, ask the class to critique it, using the SAY IT guidelines and identifying facts and examples that support the point of view.

Explain that the letters express the opinions of individual readers about the issue covered in the editorial. Read and critique the letters, using the SAY IT (p. 215) guidelines and identifying facts and examples that support the point of view. (Note: Letter 2 is missing supporting facts and examples.) Then have small groups critique the editorials and letters in the Subject Folders you prepared earlier.

➡ Follow Up

Ask students to work independently or with a partner to write an editorial on a current issue about which they have strong feelings and opinions. Post editorials on a bulletin board and encourage students to write and post letters to the editor that support or counter the editorial opinion.

Tip Act as a mentor during the groups' discussions. When appropriate, help students pinpoint specific words and phrases that back up their critiques of the editorials and letters.

Persuasive Writing

Name _____ Date _____

Persuading for Different Purposes:
WRITING EDITORIALS AND LETTERS

EDITORIAL

To what extent should drivers of all-terrain vehicles determine how our woodlands are used? This is a question that concerns all of us who like to explore the Catskill Mountains. Here at the *Mountain Post,* we believe that our forests and hills attract residents and tourists who like hiking through the wild, untouched beauty and silence of the woods and hills. We feel that all-terrain vehicles destroy these attractions. The vehicles are noisy. Drivers cut muddy paths through forests, destroying plants and frightening animals away. The question of access to our woodlands is currently before our state legislators. We urge all of you to who love the wilderness of our mountains to write to our state representatives. Urge them to conserve our hills by prohibiting vehicles.

1. To the Editor:

Your comments about all-terrain vehicles in woodlands are way off-base! First of all, state parks are open to everyone, and there's no law on the books that says drivers can't use the parks. Second, most of the drivers I know are really careful not to disturb or destroy wild growth and animal habitats.

As for noise, I don't think vehicles make any more noise than do hikers who are always talking and yelling. Also, drivers who go into remote areas of the mountains often find lost hikers or dangerous situations. Like lifeguards, we report these situations to the park rangers.

Tiry Wheelgood
Petunsquet, New York

2. To the Editor:

My family enjoys using mountain bikes and ski-mobiles in the hills. We don't agree with your editorial. Other people who feel as we do should write their state representatives.

Ike Biker
Snowville, New York

Persuading for Different Purposes: WRITING CRITICAL REVIEWS- BOOK REVIEWS

Goal: Practice using persuasive strategies in writing a book review.

➡ Get Set

In general, a book report simply supplies data. A book review, on the other hand, analyzes and evaluates a work of literature and tells the reviewer's opinion of it.

➡ Go

Start with a discussion of word meanings.

Everyday Talk: *Criticize* and *Criticism* usually mean pointing out negative points. Examples: *He criticized my clothes by saying they were out-of-date. His constant criticism of my clothes made me feel awful.*

The Language of Reviewers: *Criticize, Criticism, Critique,* and *Critical* mean analyzing and evaluating something, stressing the strong, positive points as well as any weak points. Examples: *She helped me criticize (or critique) my story to see whether one event leads to the next one. Her criticism showed me that my story is logical. In her critical review, she praised the way I develop the personality of the main character. Her critique also suggested that the story setting was too vague.*

Distribute the reproducible on page 219, and preview the guidelines for writing book reviews. Discuss students' reactions and responses. To whom would this review be particularly helpful? What else would students like the reviewer to talk about?

➡ Follow Up

Ask each student to choose a book he or she has read to review. Then have them read aloud and discuss their reviews in small groups. Reviewers note group criticisms and decide which ones they'll implement in a final copy.

Tip Prompt group members to talk about how each review did or didn't follow the guidelines on the reproducible.

Persuasive Writing

Name _____ Date _____

Persuading for Different Purposes: WRITING CRITICAL REVIEWS– BOOK REVIEWS

BOOK REVIEWS—Guidelines for Writing a Book Review

1. Tell the title of the book, the author's name, and the reviewer's name.
   (For example, State Your Subject and tell who You, the reviewer, is.)
2. Start with a sentence that grab's your audience's attention.
   (For example, Know Your Audience.)
3. Supply details.
   - What is the book about?
   - If you've read other books by this writer, tell how this book is like or unlike them.
   - State the theme of the book: What message or idea is the writer trying to persuade readers to accept?
4. Know Your Intention. Are you recommending the book for everyone to read? Just for classmates with special interests? To no one, because you think the book has serious flaws?
5. Decide on a Tone for your report. Will you be serious? Funny? Informal? Formal? Worried? Happy?

—————————— **KIDS AT WORK by Russell Freedman** ——————————
Reviewer: Charles Reeder

Do you think history is boring? You'll change your mind when you read Russell Freedman's *Kids at Work: Lewis Hine and the Crusade Against Child Labor*. This nonfiction book tells about how thousands of kids had to do back-breaking labor in mines, mills, and factories, and how Lewis Hine, a reporter and photographer, recorded their work.

Russell Friedman is well-known for his ability to tell about history in personal ways. For example, in *The Wright Brothers*, Freedman tells how Orville and Wilbur Wright felt when their first attempts at manned flights failed. In *Kids at Work*,

Freedman shows how frustrated Hine became as he tried to get his message across to the public that young children should be in school, not in sweatshops. Yet, the theme of the book is that courage and perseverance eventually pay off. After many years, Hine's photos and articles led to child-labor laws.

Kids at Work is not an easy book to read because Freedman doesn't talk down to his audience. But the book will be valuable to you if you're interested in the problems kids faced many years ago.

Persuasive Writing

Persuading for Different Purposes:
WRITING CRITICAL REVIEWS—
FIELDS OF INTEREST

Goal: Practice using persuasive strategies in writing a critical review of places and events.

➡ Get Set

Students can apply what they've learned about critiques and book reviews to write critical reviews of places and events.

➡ Go

With students, brainstorm a list of local businesses and community events that they can critique, such as grocery stores, gas stations, fairs, museums, restaurants, book stores, playgrounds, concerts, clothing stores, drugstores, parks, and music stores.

Hand out the reproducible on page 221. Review the information in Section A about critiquing a restaurant and a county fair. Have the class choose one or two items from their brainstormed list and think of some features a critique should tell about.

➡ Follow Up

Direct pairs to choose an example for one of the items to critique, such as a local restaurant.

Tip To conference and suggest revisions, writing groups can use the following questions as guidelines:
- Does the critique follow the SAY IT guidelines?
- Does the critique supply specific details?
- Is the reviewer's opinion or rating clear?
- Is one critique more convincing than the other? If so, why?

Persuasive Writing

Name _____ Date _____

Persuading for Different Purposes:
WRITING CRITICAL REVIEWS–
FIELDS OF INTEREST

A. You can write critical reviews of places and events, too. Here's a critical review of a clothing store.

A New Clothing Store

There's a new store on Main Street. It's Jan's Jeans 'n' Stuff, a small shop packed with many name brands of clothing and shoes.

My friends and I visited the store on opening day to see if it carried our favorite kind of athletic shoes, Road Hogs. No such luck, but we did find racks and shelves packed with the kinds of T-shirts, jeans, caps, and baseball jackets we like. The prices are a little higher than they are at Soupy Savers. However, Soupy Savers doesn't have the variety that Jan's Jeans does. Also, we were impressed by the great service at Jan's. The clerks are polite and helpful. If you're looking for the latest in casual clothes, I suggest you give Jan's a try.

B. Look at the features that a critique of a restaurant and a county fair might contain.

Restaurant	County Fair
atmosphere type of food quality of food prices service	purpose or sponsors kinds of rides and attractions transportation, parking costs and fees safety
Reviewer's Rating:	**Reviewer's Rating:**
Do you recommend this restaurant? Why or why not?	Do you encourage others to go to the fair? Why or why not?

C. Now it's your turn to write a critique about a place or event.

Persuasive Writing

Persuasive Writing

Persuading for Different Purposes: THINKING ABOUT YOUR AUDIENCE

> Goal: Predict and counter the supporting reasons for an opposing point of view.

➡ Get Set

In the Thinking About Your Audience lesson on page 194–195, students objectively listed pro and con positions on an issue. This activity extends the concept and skill for your students: they not only try to *predict* the supporting reasons for an opposing point of view, but also *counter* these reasons as they write their persuasive paragraphs or essays.

➡ Go

Distribute the reproducible on page 223. Have students work in groups of five or six and explain their task:

- In Section 1, each group lists at least three reasons to support a No-Homework policy. Explain that while they're working, you'll also be listing three reasons that support a Pro-Homework policy on a piece of paper.
- After the groups complete Section 1, they confer to predict your reasons for supporting a Pro-Homework policy. The group enters its predictions in Section 2.

➡ Follow Up

Read aloud one group's responses to Sections 1 and 2, and your reasons for supporting the Pro-Homework policy. Work with the class to respond to Our Opponent's Position by phrasing statements (counterarguments) for Section 3, and tell students to write the counterarguments in the section.

> **Tip** While students may wish to tell how their groups' entries tally with the examples you read aloud, stress that different entries may also be valid. Point out that while we can't always predict exactly what the opposition may say, we can make some good guesses to counter their views.

Persuasive Writing

Name _____ Date _____

Persuading for Different Purposes:
THINKING ABOUT YOUR AUDIENCE

PROS AND CONS ABOUT HOMEWORK

1. Our Position: Our school should have a No-Homework policy. Here are the supporting reasons for our point of view.

_____

_____

_____

_____

_____

_____

2. Our Opponent's Position: Here are our opponent's reasons for supporting a Pro-Homework policy.

_____

_____

_____

_____

_____

_____

3. Counterarguments: Here are our group's ideas for countering, or answering, the arguments and supporting reasons of our opponent in #2.

_____

_____

_____

_____

_____

_____

Persuasive Writing

Persuading for Different Purposes:
WRITING A PERSUASIVE ESSAY

> **Goal:** Develop a four-paragraph persuasive essay.

➡ Get Set

Explain that an essay is a broad term that refers to a short composition on a single subject. In a persuasive essay, the writer states his or her point of view on a subject and gives reasons for holding this point of view.

➡ Go

Distribute the reproducibles on pages 225 and 226. Begin by reviewing the skills at the bottom of page 225. Then explain that the outline at the top shows the form of the persuasive essay, and that page 226 presents a sample persuasive essay.

Ask pairs to explore topics for their own persuasive essays. Most students will find ideas and writing samples in their Writing Folders that they can develop into essays. Stress that students should pick a topic about which there are genuine differences of opinion.

➡ Follow Up

Provide several writing periods for students to plan, polish, and present their essays. As a prewriting strategy, loosen up students by having them freewrite for three or four minutes about their topic. The drafting stage involves two steps:

Step One: Make an outline, following the model on the reproducible. If you wish, go over the outline with a writing partner and ask for input and suggestions. You may want to revise your outline.

Step Two: Use your outline as a guide to write your first draft. Put it away for a day. Return to it and add fresh ideas and changes. **Conference** with your writing partner to solve any specific problems in the essay. Revise your essay. Work with your partner to proofread for errors in grammar, spelling, and punctuation. Make the **final copy**.

> **Tip** Write a persuasive essay to show students. After reading each paragraph aloud, pause to get students' input about the skills and guidelines you used. Build an I-Can-Do-That-Too atmosphere by reminding students that they've already practiced and applied each skill.

Name _____ Date _____

Persuading for Different Purposes:
WRITING A PERSUASIVE ESSAY

Outline for a Persuasive Essay

I. Introductory Paragraph

    A. State your subject and your intention in writing about it. Identify yourself and the audience you're addressing.

    B. Give **two** reasons that support your argument.

    C. State your opinion in just a sentence or two.

II. Development Paragraph

    A. Restate the **first** reason that supports your point of view.

    B. Write sentences that give examples and details that support this reason.

III. Development Paragraph

    A. Restate the **second** reason that supports your point of view.

    B. Write sentences that give examples and details that support this reason.

IV. Concluding Paragraph

    A. Restate the subject of your essay.

    B. Summarize how your reasons support your point of view.

    C. Conclude with a summary of your opinion.

Skills That Will Help You Write a Successful Persuasive Essay:

- stating your subject clearly
- stating your opinion
- using logic and reasoning
- choosing a tone
- identifying yourself
- using facts and examples
- considering your audience
- using exact, vivid words

P.S. See the essay "Mall Manners" for a sample of persuasive writing.

100 Writing Lessons © by Tara McCarthy • Scholastic Teaching Resources

Persuasive Writing

Name _____ Date _____

Persuading for Different Purposes:
WRITING A PERSUASIVE ESSAY

SAMPLE MODEL ESSAY: MALL MANNERS

Like most other people in our community, I like the stores, food court, and CinePlex at Mathis Mall. But one problem at the mall has been a bunch of rowdy kids. The mall management has just hired two Roving Ambassadors to help solve the problem. I support the management's decision. The rowdy kids scare shoppers and make them angry. Also, most of the kids involved are really insecure and are looking for someone to respect them.

Most of us who go to the mall want to shop and eat in peace. We don't like to be alarmed or threatened by kids who are pushing, shoving, skating, hollering, and running around bumping into people. In fact, this kind of behavior makes some of us shoppers so angry that we stop going to the mall. The Roving Ambassadors will solve this problem by spotting troublemakers and escorting them outside.

Both Roving Ambassadors are people who like kids and understand their problems. Some kids just need an adult who will tell them what the rules are. Mall rules are simple: come here only to shop, eat, or see movies. Some kids also need to find positive ways of getting attention. The Roving Ambassadors will point out some positive ways, like opening doors for elderly people and cleaning up after oneself at the food court.

Malls are designed to be inviting to everyone in the community. Roving Ambassadors will keep our mall peaceful by identifying troublemakers and taking them aside. The ambassadors will help these kids by stating rules and by sharing ideas about how to get attention in ways that get praise, not blame. I think the idea of Roving Ambassadors is one that will benefit all of us.

Persuading for Different Purposes: WIND-UP

Distribute the reproducible on page 227, and ask a volunteer to read aloud the persuasive essay titled "Homework: Yes!" Remind students that they completed a reproducible (p. 223) that dealt with the issue of homework. Challenge them to use that page and the reproducible on page 225 to help them compose a persuasive essay that counters "Homework: Yes!" Allow at least two class periods for students to prepare an outline and draft an essay. Encourage writing partners to work together to critique each other's work and to make revisions based on those conversations.

Persuasive Writing

Name _____ Date _____

Persuading for Different Purposes: WIND-UP

After reading this persuasive essay, take the opposite side and write a persuasive essay titled "Homework: No!"

Homework: Yes!

A debate is raging about the value of homework for students in our school system. This debate involves a conflict among students, teachers, and parents. As a student in Room 10 at Flora Daski Middle School, I'm pro-homework. Homework takes up a lot of my time, but it also encourages me to develop my interests and to get my family involved in interesting projects.

I have some interests that are tied into school subjects. One of my main interests is collecting historical, antique American coins and paper money. Opponents of homework may think I can pursue this interest at school, but actually I rely on school history lessons to inspire after-school quests for rare items that I could never find at school! For example, our teacher assigned our class to find examples of things used in pre-revolutionary days in America. So after school, I went to the local historical museum and found examples of paper money used in Thomas Jefferson's day. Away from school, I found examples to show to my classmates.

Some opponents of homework claim that it interferes with free time with your family. Actually, I've found that an interesting homework assignment can get you more involved with your family. For example, the homework assignments to find persuasive strategies in TV commercials got my whole family involved in critiquing commercials. We had fun detecting persuasive techniques and shared a lot of ideas as we discussed them.

In conclusion, I support homework assignments that help you go on learning away from school. Opponents of homework don't realize that learning is not confined to the classroom. I vote for homework that encourages my interests and helps me and my family learn together!

Persuasive Writing

Name _____ Date _____

On Your Own: THE BAD GUYS SPEAK!

Brainstorm a list of villains from folktales and fairy tales. (Remember, Snow White's stepmother? How about the giant in "Jack and the Beanstalk"?) Choose one of the bad guys. Write a paragraph that tells the story from his or her point of view.

Share your work with classmates. How does this new viewpoint add to their understanding of the original story?

100 Writing Lessons © by Tara McCarthy • Scholastic Teaching Resources

Persuasive Writing

Name _____ Date _____

On Your Own: WRITE A DECLARATION

The last sentence of the second paragraph of the Declaration of Independence reads:

"The history of the present King of Great Britain is a history of repeated injuries and usurpations, all having in direct object the establishment of an absolute tyranny over these States. To prove this, let facts be submitted to a candid world."

Then Thomas Jefferson listed 27 facts and examples to prove the point!

What issue at school or home concerns you? Write your own Declaration on the issue. Follow these guidelines:

- The first part of the Declaration should present your point of view.
- The next part of the Declaration should present at least three facts that support your point of view.
- The last part of the Declaration should suggest a solution.

Persuasive Writing

Name _____ Date _____

On Your Own:
IMPOSSIBLE ADS–UNSTACKING THE CARDS

Imagine that all advertisers actually want to present not only the best qualities of their own product but also the best qualities of their competitor's product. Here's an example:

> Movie Munches are the crunchiest, yummiest chocolate snacks you'll ever find for chomping on at your local CinePlex. You chocolate lovers will adore our melty, down-home, silk-on-your-tongue flavor. On the other hand, if you don't like chocolate, or are allergic to it, buy a bunch of our competitor's Viewer Veggies. These wholesome snacks are chocolate-free and are made out of nourishing broccoli and sun-dried tomatoes.

Look at the ads you've written for this section. Rewrite them to include a competitor's selling points.

Persuasive Writing

Name _____ Date _____

On Your Own:
A DEBATE BETWEEN BOOK CHARACTERS

With a partner, choose two characters from two different books or stories and imagine them debating an issue or exchanging opinions. For instance, the wolf from "Little Red Riding Hood" and the fox from "The Fox and the Grapes" might talk about the best meal each has ever had.

Present your debate as a written conversation or set it up as a dialogue for a skit. And remember—apply the SAY IT guidelines as you develop the debate.

100 Writing Lessons © by Tara McCarthy • Scholastic Teaching Resources

Persuasive Writing

Name _____ Date _____

100 Writing Lessons © by Tara McCarthy • Scholastic Teaching Resources

On Your Own:
DETECTING ARGUMENT FALLACIES

Watch television discussion shows at home with your family. Can you detect any of the following common "argument fallacies"? (A *fallacy* is an error in reasoning.) Make a chart of your findings that includes the name of the TV show, the speakers, and which "argument fallacy" they presented.

- **The Missing the Point fallacy:** The speaker expresses an opinion, but then offers facts that have nothing to do with the opinion. For example: "The residents need flood relief immediately. This is a wonderful part of the country, and our governor is a fine man."

- **The Ad Hominem fallacy:** The speaker doesn't address the issue, but instead attacks his or her opponent personally. For example: "I disagree with you about school uniforms. You're a dangerous person who's always trying to change everything."

- **Circular Reasoning:** The speaker tries to support an idea by stating the same idea in a different way. For example: "You should eat healthy foods because they're good for you. The reason they're good for you is because they're healthy."

Persuasive Writing

Name _____ Date _____

On Your Own: RATE YOURSELF

1. For you, what's the most challenging or hardest thing about persuasive writing?

_____

_____

_____

_____

2. For you, what's the easiest thing about persuasive writing?

_____

_____

_____

_____

3. Of all the persuasive writing you've done in this section, which piece pleases you the most? Why?

_____

_____

_____

4. Of all the persuasive writing you've done in this section, which pleases you the least? Why?

_____

_____

_____

_____

100 Writing Lessons © by Tara McCarthy • Scholastic Teaching Resources

Composition: TRANSITIONAL WORDS

In persuasive writing, a writer may present opposing ideas to state his or her viewpoint. Share the following examples with students:

> *A weekend curfew for teenagers might make our town quieter at night, <u>however</u>, a curfew might violate young people's rights.*
>
> *A weekend curfew for teenagers might make our town quieter at night, <u>but</u> a curfew might violate young people's rights.*
>
> *A weekend curfew for teenagers might make our town quieter at night. <u>On the other hand</u>, a curfew might violate young people's rights.*
>
> *A weekend curfew for teenagers might make our town quieter at night—<u>although</u> a curfew might violate young people's rights.*

Point out that using certain transitional words and phrases such as *however, but, on the other hand,* and *although* can help the writer make the case.

Distribute the reproducible on page 236 to students. Go over the list of transitional words and phrases and the examples.

More Practice

Supply some sentence frames and ask the class to provide transitional words and phrases from the list on the reproducible. Here are some suggestions:

Some school-board members believe that schools should be in session all year 'round; (<u>however</u> or <u>but</u>) most students and many teachers oppose the idea.

Students should not have to do homework (<u>unless</u>) they haven't completed their work in class.

My mom thinks billboards are an ugly blight on the landscape. (<u>In contrast</u>, <u>On the other hand</u>), my dad believes billboards are helpful to travelers and local businesses.

Persuasive Writing

Name _____ Date _____

Composition: TRANSITIONAL WORDS

Transitional words and phrases show how ideas are connected. Writers use transitional words and phrases when they're presenting opposing ideas.

although	**but**	**however**	**in contrast**
though	**unlike**	**yet**	**on the other hand**
the reverse	**while**	**unless**	

EXAMPLES:

- Many people feel that all students should play sports, <u>but</u> many other people feel that students should be able to substitute another activity.
- <u>Unlike</u> most of my classmates, I believe that students should be given more homework.
- Families on vacation want to visit national parks, <u>yet</u> many of these parks are damaged by an overload of tourist traffic.
- <u>While</u> many people argue that capital punishment cuts down on crime, other people argue <u>the reverse</u>, that it doesn't cut down on crime at all.

Look over the persuasive writing you've done for this part of the book. How can you use transitional words and phrases to make your point more clearly and strongly?

100 Writing Lessons © by Tara McCarthy • Scholastic Teaching Resources

Composition: USING EXACT WORDS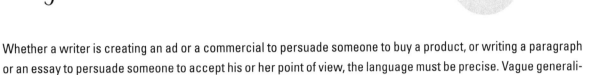

Whether a writer is creating an ad or a commercial to persuade someone to buy a product, or writing a paragraph or an essay to persuade someone to accept his or her point of view, the language must be precise. Vague generalities won't persuade many people in the audience.

Write the following chart on the board or display it on the overhead. For each pair, ask students to identify the ad that will be more appealing to a savvy audience, and to explain their choice.

1. Basketball Bouncers are great!	Basketball Bouncers are durable, support your feet, and meet the newest standards for hip kids' design.
2. Wizard Electronics will refund your purchase price and add a 50% bonus if you find a lower price in a competing store.	Visit Wizard Electronics for low prices and friendly service. After all, we've been your neighbor for 27 years!
3. Go With the Glow that never fades! A built-in recharger automatically repowers your Glowworm flashlight when the batteries run low.	Everybody wants to conquer the Glow-Light Glowworm. But nobody can beat the Glowworm for dependability. Go with the Glowworm!

More Practice

Distribute the reproducible on page 238. Help students identify the general words in the web (those in capital letters) and then ask them to find specific and exact phrases that tell why Homework Honcho is practical and time-saving. Challenge students to complete the web by suggesting phrases that would make the other web entries more exact.

Persuasive Writing

Name _____ Date _____

Composition: USING EXACT WORDS

In order to persuade an audience to buy a product or accept your opinion, you must use precise and exact words. The web shows some general categories for persuading someone to buy the product, Homework Honcho. Complete the web by using exact words to make the categories more detailed and convincing.

100 Writing Lessons © by Tara McCarthy • Scholastic Teaching Resources

Across the Curriculum:
WRITING ABOUT MATH

People can register their views in reviews, editorials, letters to the editor—and in surveys. The results of surveys can then be displayed in charts and graphs.

A few days before teaching this activity, ask students to look through newspapers and magazines to find charts or graphs that illustrate poll results of public opinion on a current problem, issue, or debate. Begin the activity by showing the charts and graphs on the overhead. Discuss the following questions:

- What question or questions did poll respondents have to answer?
- What different opinions does the visual show?
- How are responses shown on the visual?
- What opinion does the majority of respondents hold?
- Do you think the visual is accurate or misleading? Why?

Have the class work together to compose a paragraph that summarizes the opinions in one of the graphs or charts that students brought in. Remind students that the first sentence should state what the issue is.

Examples:
- People who live in public housing have different opinions about whether residents should be allowed to keep dogs.
- There's a big debate going on about whether our schools should require students to wear uniforms.

Write About Math

Have students conduct their own surveys about a current school or community issue. Distribute the reproducible on page 240 for survey guidelines.

Persuasive Writing

Name _____ Date _____

Across the Curriculum:
WRITING ABOUT MATH

Conduct a survey about a current school or community issue. Think about these questions:

- How will you phrase the survey questions so that they are clear?
- Whom will you interview to make sure you get a variety of opinions?
- How will you tally and record the responses?
- How will you display the results—on a graph or a chart?

THE ISSUE IS:

_____

_____

_____

MY SURVEY QUESTION IS:

_____

_____

_____

On a separate piece of paper, display the results in a graph or a chart—and write a summary of them.